NO MORE TRAUMA !

Simple steps to reset TRAUMA using George Booty's amazing 'Virtual Brain Reset'.

George A. Booty

Kindle Publishing

CONTENTS

NO MORE TRAUMA ! – *Simple steps to reset TRAUMA using George Booty's Amazing*   ©'*Virtual*
Brain Re-Set ™*!*

First published by Kindle Direct Publishing. Published in contract with Kindle Direct Publishing. Printed in Poland by Amazon Fulfillment. Poland Sp. Zo.o., Wroclaw.

Published in part, in January 2013, as Seminar notes to students, *shown then as,*
TRAUMA, FEARS & PHOBIAS – Identifying and Dealing with Trauma. Convergence College of Psycho-therapy Productions. Milton Keynes. England. UK.

MEDICAL DISCLAIMER: The following information is intended for general information purposes only. Individuals should always see their main health care provider, such as their GP, or their licensed psychotherapist, or psychotraumatologist, before administering any suggestions made in this book. This is due to the fact that the author has no personal knowledge of the sufferer without personal involvement in their particular case history. Any application of the material set forth in the following pages is at the reader's discretion and is his or her sole responsibility. The author takes full responsibility for representing and interpreting the ideas related to the various theories remarked upon and the training carried out at Convergence College. The author's interpretations and representations may vary in intent and accuracy from the original writings and presentations by the respective author's theories of psychology, such as the giants of the past, whose shoulders we stand upon, namely, the other professors, masters, theorists, psychiatrists, clinicians, or gifted tutors, which were responsible for the many theories and developments, culminating in what we have learned about and utilised in these various forms of psychotherapies and in the simple psychological techniques used, in attempting to treat Trauma and therefore offering truly hopeful means of therapy, to patients, or clients, around the world.

Library of Congress Cataloguing in Publication Data
Booty, George A.

   NO MORE TRAUMA ! - *Simple steps to reset TRAUMA using George Booty's Amazing* '*Virtual*
   Brain Re-Set'!

   Bibliography: p.

         1.   Psychotherapy. 1. Booty, George.
         2.   II. Title.
         3.   **ISBN:** 9781089565116.

Kindle Direct Publishing

INTRODUCTION

If you only have a hammer, everything seems like a nail.

~Rumi.

My intention here is to inform Major TRAUMA sufferers there is **New Hope**! There is no need to settle for a life of suffering with all the pain of Major Trauma. Real help is seriously here.

I recall a sketched image, presented, at a Ra, Ra! Meeting, as a sales manager, in my former life. The drawing was ironic. It was meant to encourage salesmen/women everywhere, not to take no for an answer. It shows a scene, set in early America, at the time of the Indian wars, being engaged by General Custer's men on a scouting expedition to protect settlers.

The picture shows a troop of cavalry soldiers, using old single shot rifles and inaccurate six guns, while surrounded by very ferocious native American Indians, who were circling the soldiers and with much skill, very effectively, raining arrows down on them with great accuracy. The picture, sadly showing, many of the soldiers, were already dead. At the same time at the rear, there is a salesman with a covered wagon. Timidly, trying to talk to the Major in charge, on the salesman's wagon, is a brand new 'Gatling gun' (a machine gun) that was able to fire zillions of bullets, at great speed and the 'Major's assistant, is nonchalantly saying. *"Look, will you just Go away! The Major is very busy, can't you see, this is life and death here, and we do not have time to look at this new invention of yours, we are being overrun!?".*

Writing this book entitled '**NO MORE TRAUMA**' will hopefully inform anyone who reads it, about the new

kid on the block (no gun intended) which is our latest therapy called '*NeuroSomaSocioPsychoSpiritual*' *(NSSPS) System,* which was developed at the Convergence College of Psychotherapy, in England, UK.
FAST RELIEF is available now

I believe this book will bring the opportunity for fast relief for all types of major psychological TRAUMA sufferers, including those sufferers with lesser traumatic fears and phobias, bringing fast and effective solutions (my aim is to concretise the facts here) to let everyone know, that sufferers may gain complete relief and *No More Trauma* energy experienced.

We may remove the trapped shock, not with a gun, but with our latest methods. Once a patient has experienced our effective treatments, where we use unique and very modern developments, with advances in neuroscience, somatic bodywork, socio relational schemas, psychological resistance of inbuilt defence mechanisms and there may be times of spiritual peace, for those who find they may plug into it, if not, the spiritual aspect can just be left to one side. This is where our Convergence treatment models, offer incredibly wide, holistic and very effective methods and most importantly, we get very fast results in our Trauma work. It works for all.

It is with professional pride we are able to celebrate our very unique © *Virtual Brain Re-Set*^{TM} therapy for all Traumas.

You will find hope here

If you wish to find relief or help others you will find hope here. I shall explain more about Trauma relief for sufferers and some of our case histories including the way we work (all names and specific circumstances were changed to protect individuals) and for those interested to learn more, we supply further details of the training offered within the main body of this book.

How do we know any Trauma treatment works?

Unsurprisingly, we have been helping major Trauma sufferers, at the popular local *Psycho-TRAUMA*

Surgery, in Milton Keynes and at our *Lifescript Clinic of Harley Street* (London) clinic for many years.

We need to be sure there is an honest evidence base regarding the results of this treatment we offer.

So how do we know if a trauma has been resolved? It is simply not enough to attend the referral treatments, such as tfCBT, or Mindfulness, or any other relatively ineffective Major Trauma treatments, signposted from the GP, where there is no credible evidence that a Trauma has been fully dealt with, or a Trauma has been removed and is no longer causing problems (instead of only being reduced slightly in intensity, for a while).

Trauma sufferers do not need a sticking plaster.
We need to know exactly what has changed?

Well, some administrators and those in charge of mental health treatments in UK, may say this, "*the counsellor or the psychologist reports that the client has 'ticked the box' to say they are 'feeling a bit better than they did before'.*".

We say, "*Really! in what way?*", and "*How much better are they?*"

Maybe there is a slight calming, but the Trauma has not GONE...!

The questions we must be prepared to ask are;

"*Has the Traumatic trapped shock been removed altogether and the symptoms gone?*".

"*Can the person, after therapy, do the things they could not do before the PTSD?*".

"*Have the symptoms left and not returned?*".

We also take this opportunity to encourage and applaud, the many great therapists, around Great Britain and beyond, who perform Trauma *'resolution'* solutions administered by *'removing' the trapped shock* for their patient's. This is true trauma resolution, when there is a full return to a normal systemic vagal health response, unless the work is ongoing and very complex, in those cases, there is a healing curve that is truly noticeable, to both patient and clinician.

We must also recognise the compassion for all patients, whom caring therapist's treat as individuals, in the real sense of the word (as a 'unique person') rather than treating a purely diagnostic related and purely clinical 'symptom' or 'illness' that perhaps had been prompted by reading the DSM-V or ICD-10 psychiatric medical models.

Many now believe these psychiatric labels are not helping, as they are not working very well for patients; and furthermore we believe this psychiatric diagnosis programme is considered to be continually failing the suffering people, both in the West and also elsewhere around the world.

Please understand this book, is therefore born out of my personal heartfelt concerns and frustration, over the lack of Trauma information supplied to sufferers, regarding the availability of, up to date, life changing and complete 'Trauma Therapy resolutions' largely on offer by many truly informed, highly trained and therefore, very skilled, modern psychotherapists and qualified psychotraumatologists, currently offering complete and effective treatment in this area.

Waiting Times for Trauma Treatments

The waiting times for Trauma therapy in England right now is exacerbating the problem and squeezing patients into this failing system of labelling and treatment plans, while they await the treatment and the powerful drugs prescribed by the psychiatrists' whom often prescribe these dreadful drugs to their poor traumatised and suffering patients This is happening all the time now within the NHS; it is generally recognised that GP's are the biggest drug dealers and pushers in the world.

Big Drug Money Involved

Well I may be unpopular with the Medical world to say this, but there is a great deal of *money in pharmaceutical drugs*, which is also not helped by the waiting times for treatments of the real Mental Health Issues (currently nine months waiting here for CBT and for specialised Major Trauma treatment such as EMDR it is much longer and therefore it brings desperation as that makes it quite elusive to many sufferers (it is currently upwards of 18 months in Milton Keynes, Buckinghamshire) at the time of writing.

Our NHS is Great

I know that workers within the NHS, do a great job on the whole and I am not here to simply knock the NHS, as in many areas they help a lot of people. We know about the unsung heroes, the mundane work of the maintenance staff and for those who work as nurses, doctors, surgeons, etc, and all the other associated disciplines, are essentially caring and hard-working individuals, many of whom obviously love their work, looking after others and feel deeply for their patients. There are a great many human beings with big hearts.

Thank you NHS workers (Big Clap!)

So I want to say, a big thank you, to all of those people in the NHS right now, who work tirelessly, in saving lives, especially, but also to those who do mundane jobs in surgeries and hospitals, to make our quality of life better in this country. Also to the care homes and care workers who visit the old and infirm.

All is not lost

The good news is that, at the same time of this current NHS crisis, regarding therapy help for mental health sufferers, other private professionals are poised waiting in the wings and ready to help major Trauma sufferers around the UK.

This has all come about, by our newer understanding, mainly through neuroscience; along with continued research and the great many altruistic and independent mental health workers, always contributing experiences and new methods, that have developed since the early days of psychotherapy theory advances.

As a trainee psychotherapist, I distinctly recall, hearing an explanation that proposed, in effect,

"that Trauma clients will probably arrive and be an issue for you, that you may well have to deal with, once you graduate and become a psychotherapist. This type of Traumatised client is usually considered very long term, some have been in therapy for over thirty years or more, which is simply a matter of regular support and psychological holding and waiting, for time to heal, that poor unfortunate person" And *"this is the Trauma sufferer's only hope in therapy – time alone can heal them"*, this is what I clearly recall being told.

It was further explained, there is another stronger treatment used by the mental health service called ECT, and is for those patients who seem to have lost their way completely and possibly confused, anxious and manically depressed, and in an almost catatonic state, or suffering violent or psychotic episodes, which is where psychiatrists administer 'Electric Shock Treatment', which we feel is quite barbaric in this day and age, although some elderly sufferers suggest it has improved their lives by literally 'jolting' them back to reality and normality of life.

The electrical voltage administered, shocks the brain and in laymen's, or computer speak, terms, causes the brain to physically reboot again, not unlike the paramedic's 'Defibrillators' (Crash equipment) used to restart the heart.

So, as students, we were told in similar disclosures, that it is right to continue to counsel the Traumatised clients (as they need help) simply using the talking cure. *'But naturally anything really bad, like shell-shock and other terrors of the mind, like major personality disorders or schizophrenia, are dealt with by the psychiatrists and specialist psychologists, within a hospital setting, for everyone's safety'.*

The main excuse, suggesting we do not need to refer, to in depth psychiatric help, unless there is extreme difficulty in session (they have usually had that help already and it failed them). But also being told, *"originally, these types of patients, like those with major mental illness were previously held in a secure mental hospital, to safeguard the public, and many were just contained, even against their own will, within old buildings we called Sanatoriums".*

"Therefore, because these institutions are no longer around today, we may just have to offer support for this type of patient as well, but as an aside they explained, don't expect much to change with their trauma problem, it just takes time and we have to trust that time will heal in the end!".

This was the therapy suggested and the prognosis for trauma clients, presented to me and sadly, I totally believed it to begin with, until I learned differently for myself when I continued to research and learn and eventually studied psycho-Trauma more thoroughly.

Obviously, this is the hand of cards, which many trained counsellors, psychologists, psychiatrists and mental health workers and in some cases, even psychotherapists like myself, have been dealt, within professional training, which is ludicrous because it is so outdated in content.

Discussion around major Trauma was always guarded (for fear of bringing too much personal stuff up) and somehow because it was not apparently our remit in psychotherapy training, there was never any helpful discussions to know why, when, how, or even information on, where, to 'refer', onto a specialist clinician.

But I realised later that there is a great deal of professional jealousy between the psychiatric / psychology medical science side and the psychotherapy treatments craft side which explains the idea of it all being separated out. Egos are at stake here big time. Yet through training in Trauma, fortunately I found out there is also a lot we may do in psychotherapy with Trauma patients and in real terms we may see them healed much faster and with very little re-traumatising necessary.

In fact with my modern ©*Virtual Brain Re-Set* Therapy we do not even need to know the patient's Trauma details at all, to help them reduce Trauma energy, particularly if these areas are too painful to approach in the beginning.

We are ready to offer immediate relief from these impacting events by the Convergence Psychotherapy methods of Trauma control and healing for so many poor sufferers. The question on the top of my Harley Street business card is '*Why suffer in silence?*'

Our patients may easily *access immediate life changing help* (not simple Counselling, like behavioural therapy - which will not easily *remove 'trapped' shock* for the majority. Sufferers may instantly find relief by some transformational work, bringing real and lasting peace.

There is a big problem that must be addressed within the existing mental health service and that is to understand we need to get away from the medical models that are failing and have a complete rethink.

One size does not fit everyone and that is the basis of why we say Trauma specialists need to be psychotherapists first to understand the deeper psychological issues underlying each person whom has been traumatised and know how to deal with people in a different way. You need people training and life skills to be able to do that.

For example; I have spoken to many very clever graduates, with first degrees and even those with master's degree in psychology who explain to me honestly, that they "do not have a clue how to apply the knowledge they have to the patients!". Unfortunately, psychology is not taught in that experiential way.

At Convergence we have a heart for those who are suffering and want to help them and that is why we have worked so hard to refine this field of Trauma therapy. We are very different from the mainstream NHS model, as we are seeking to establish a fresh look at the diagnostic models used previously and suggest we do not need a new diagnostic model, rather what we really need is a 'new framework of reference that is non-diagnostic'.

We need something that reflects real people and not statistical nonsense that may cause people labelled by it to feel more harm than good. The existing DSM-5 in USA and the ICD-10 (ICD-11 due out) is facing a lot of problems today. We really do need to understand that these issues of distress and forms of presenting are not best understood to be medical illnesses.

To that end I will show below the many useful tools in the psychotherapists bag of intervention and life skills. These are the tools we use in the *NeuroSomaSocioPsychoSpiritual'* System. Our new system involves many skills, here are just some of the ways we are working with patients today.

Emotional intelligence, goal setting, life scripts, Dream interpretation, Waking dream work, resolving depression, By-Pass Therapy, the Rewind Technique, Mindfulness Based Mind Management, NAP motivation, Solution focus, Guided Inductions, Resolving addiction, Epigenetics, Mapping the Mindset, Bodywork symbols, Polyvagal theory, Reticular activating system (RAS), Secondary gain, Breath and Sound, Primal Scream, Psycho-Drama, Emotional Freedom (EFT), Trauma resolution, Coaching for children, Lifescripts, Treating Depression, Anxieties, Fears and Phobias, Worrying well, Day tight compartments, Convergence Psycho-Spiritual Model, SMART working, Therapeutic storytelling, Insight, Intuition, Psycho education, Suicide prevention, Affirmations, Positive mental rehearsal, ATET model, Imagery, Dissociation (DID), New paradigms, Fast track learning, Needs Assessment Formatting (NAF), Perception shifting, Self-actualisation, Positive psychology, Reframing, Metaphor, Personal empowerment, Motivational thinking, Mastery, Resilience and Resourcefulness, Human Blooming / flourishing, Anchoring, Alchemy and Relationships & Game playing, The Elemental approach, NLP Whoosh, Trauma – © 'The Virtual Brain Re-Set^{TM}*', The TIGAR test, Arts in Therapy, Aiding self-harm, Genogram family, Couples counselling, The Stop System, 'Convergence Eye Therapy' (C.E.T.), The Safe place, Safe space happiness recipe, Holistic coaching and working on the continuum of wellbeing. Many other professional theories, Tools and techniques which underpin the content of this fast paced, fast track, Convergence College of Psychotherapy programme along with, Clinician relevant Supervision.*

If you are a sufferer and only offered simple counselling help, then you really need to know about the

© *Virtual Brain Re-Set* ^{TM} Therapy, to alleviate your suffering. Contact us directly at the back of this book, for further help and to access our fully trained **Certified Convergence Clinicians**.

Our method, to reset your trapped shock to health again, is by helping that part of your brain called the 'amygdala' and is simply like restoring your computer once more. The old memory will remain, but your *trapped shock* making those memories nightmares and day-mares and flash backs, will be gone forever.

Please do not be afraid and do not worry, it is only a 'virtual' brain re-setting, and NOT a physical reset like the Electric shock treatments! There is no surgery involved, at all.

Our therapy is just like restoring a programme on your computer hard disk with an updated programme, when the old one has become corrupted, or in Trauma like a 'virus' infecting it.

The method we use, is in a therapeutic setting, done in a very relaxed way of working, to reduce the shock in your painful memories, that are causing you all the grief.

We will simply reframe them with our techniques and bring you to a place of peace and safety in session. We do not need to know all the details!

Remember that you are on a 'healing curve' once you start with us and will find things get easier even after your first session.

So get in contact directly as soon as you can, to stop the suffering and let us give you the help you need with one of our trained clinicians.

Through my personal heuristic research including my professional experience, first as a psychotherapist and secondly as a senior lecturer training students of psychotherapy, I have engaged my observing self within my involvement with ongoing Trauma work as a psychotraumatologist and supervisor of counsellors, psychotherapists and assistant psychologists, etc, and wish to continue sharing my experience to help others, hopefully through this simple book.

How our clinicians work using the © *Virtual Brain Re-Set* ™

model will be explained further. With Major Trauma (PTSD) there is a need for the Amygdala which is hot-wired through Trapped SHOCK, to be sensitively unravelled and restored to healthy functioning, by our '*Virtual Brain Re-Set*' Technique.

With kindest regards to my readers here, George Booty.

CHAPTER 1: WHAT IS TRAUMA?

There are Myths, lies, that are served up by the ignorant, or even mental health professional consultants prescribing these myths for those unfortunate sufferers, or their families.

Myth-1. That victims of Trauma have to learn to live with their Traumas for the rest of their lives.

Myth-2. The second Myth is that you just need to learn to talk about the Trauma. And it will unlock the trauma gradually over time. What debriefing actually does is to re-traumatise patients and it is non-effective in Trauma work, it literally like opening a can of worms for the untrained counsellor psychologist or therapist.

Myth-3 The Anti-depressant pill. First we have recognised that these so called Anti-depressants are not that, in truth they are in fact only *anti-anxiety* treatments and they are really *strong sleeping pills* which are really very strong drugs for the mind to deal with, so unsurprisingly they have very numbing effects and can be quite disturbing and even make people suicidal.

Myth-4 The idea that when your dog died at the age around 10 that you were really traumatised. That is not necessarily true. What effect is it having on you today? If the answer is none then it almost certainly is not a trauma.

Myth-5 The idea that someone dying of natural causes does not make you traumatised. Incorrect we are all different and what one person may take in as an uneventful occurrence, another may be traumatised by it, which is quite common

Why does someone like a journalist covering war zones, who is robust mentally, suddenly suffer from PTSD, which seems to come out of nowhere? The answer is we are all different and sometimes we are more vulnerable and things go wrong and we may pick up direct or vicarious trauma without realising the sudden impacting effect on us.

Please be assured that these statements or facts that the ignorant serve up are real Myths and I wish to bust them open right now in this book. I really want to redress this situation, as it simply is an untruth! Please read on.

The first myth to bust is that you cannot deal with the Trauma so that you get your life back. That is simply untrue. We may help you to resolve the Traumas. No matter how many there are.

Sometimes we have traumatic times through life and these traumas may be emotional hurts, or deeper psychological wounds, they may also be physical wounds, or even spiritual trauma. But first we need to establish what a Major Trauma is for us to deal with it.

When we think of trauma and we were to be asked what traumatic incidents can we think of in our lives, some are very fortunate and can only remember an experience especially in childhood, for example, when we would have been extremely upset when the family pet died, or if we lost or mislaid our blanky (piece of our old baby blanket with familiar smells, or an old piece of a nighty or tee shirt once smelling of Mummy - a transitional object)

It could be that a little teddy bear was taken away from us after several years of comfort and we stressed out a lot at that time, or maybe we felt upset the day when we found out that Father Christmas was not actually real and there was in some of these things a real felt sense of shame and foolishness at being so naïve.

Possibly we felt let down by parents and elders generally, especially if elder siblings were making fun of us about the situation and generally taking the mickey, something we all have to make peace with in this world as we cannot be so cocooned from every taunt or tease and we need to build some resilience to criticisms too.

However, these things may have been quite upsetting at the time and we could even argue the case about how traumatised we may have been at the time, when we are reminded of these things and how much effect these things had on us when we were much younger.

However, although this may have been quite sad for us at the time and feelings of fear and distrust and even abandonment in certain scenarios may have been pertinent at the time, these are not what we are referring to in those suffering the debilitating effects in our current Trauma therapy work here.

But let's not minimise the effects of all such traumatic events on the lives of children that may cause latter fears and phobic responses, even though they might seem quite inconsequential when we look back; but nevertheless, there may be some greater significance in our lives, in relation to some prominent Trauma issues even today, with some of these apparently innocuous situations, from way back when.

The Convergence College offer a one day seminar, (and may be added to our Online Platform soon) that deals with *Traumas, Fears & Phobias*, that help to explain the difference and what can be done with each of these three areas of therapeutic work. First, it explains, how to identify Major Trauma and we cover specific ways for counsellors and therapists to deal with and overcome fears, we teach EFT for this and explain about other types of fear interventions and Major Trauma treatment methods too. Included, is a workshop on phobic response, for those who may be suffering from phobias, or perhaps their counsellors, carers and close family members.

When we talk of major Trauma today, it is usually more about things that play a large part with, trapped shock, that is currently affecting our lives in the here and now.

Survivors or Sufferers?

Many of the symptoms and feelings I will be writing about here, are common for PTSD and Complex PTSD Trauma sufferers. Obviously they are sufferers that want to see themselves as survivors. However, without proper Trauma Therapy these poor unfortunate people will continue to be sufferers and not survivors. *Why suffer in Silence?*

Living with and enduring Major Trauma, is not a normal life experience, or perhaps more aptly put, it is certainly not a healthy life experience, and therefore the consequences it creates are different and hard to cope with, both in and out of relationships, yet may be deemed very normal for what the sufferers have experienced and endured thus far.

Not every survivor will endure all these symptoms, and there are other symptoms that can also be experienced. I always suggest that, If you see this difference and any of the symptoms I am writing of, please encourage the person you see suffering, to get professional help from a qualified Psychotraumatologist, straight away and not just to see a counsellor or anybody who is not a Trauma specialist. Bite the bullet and pay for the best you can afford – it pays dividends in the long run.

Joan

Here is an example of two women who suffered Trauma. They were both suffering from rape, in the first instance, a young woman we shall call Joan, at 19, was forcibly raped on her bed, one week before she contacted me for help with her Trauma, and we removed the impacting horror of shock energy, she was healed enough in just one session and was therefore able to resume studies back in the University by the following week and will go on to continue her life as a survivor and will get stronger.

Rachel

Another, was an elderly lady of 72 we shall call Rachel, whom had experienced Rape Trauma, early in life, as a young woman of 17, so she had carried the trapped energy for 60 years, which she explained sadly, that had continually plagued and affected her marriage and much later, even other relationships were affected and in her emotional life generally. She too, was healed from those impacting shock issues in just one session but had been a sufferer all her life and although was still alive, she had sadly not been a survivor, in the true sense of a healed life.

Rachel is now a survivor, with the Trauma fully removed and the memories are now faded, but because the help was not there when the event happened, she knows, she has wasted so much time, being a sufferer.

Please don't make that same mistake. Seek the help and be a sufferer who then becomes a survivor. This new therapy really works fast.

© Virtual Brain Re-Set ™ we then needed to spend some time dealing with the toxic guilt and shame felt around these Traumas and the ensuing change in philosophy regarding relationships and trust issues. This is psychotherapy treatment.

CHAPTER 2: TERMINOLOGY & DIAGNOSTICS

It appears that there are many different types of trauma.

Obviously doctors in the Accident and Emergency at hospitals are treating physical trauma all the time. Brain trauma units are constantly dealing with specific brain damage through accidents or heart stroke victims which causes is physical wounding or perhaps some sort of tumour in the brain. So a Traumatologist would work in these areas of physical wounding.

Also there are other forms of psychological trauma which a Psycho-traumatologist works in, such as the realm of the resulting consequential effects of emotional or psychological shock damage, but there are stages of Trauma too.

PTSD symptoms are usually varied and appears to show but the DSM-V gives clear criteria to look for in diagnosing PTSD. Due to copyright rules we will not be able to reproduce the published material on Post Traumatic Stress Disorder (PTSD).

This is currently recognised by the pages in the Diagnostic Manual.

DSM-5 *under Diagnostic Criteria number* **309.81** (F43.10)

It states Posttraumatic Stress Disorder criteria is recognised in adults and children older than six years of age (although children under six years of age do present symptoms but they are not covered under the adult criteria here. It continues to explain that we may recognise PTSD by understanding what usually happens to bring on these types of symptoms.

First there is the exposure to death, which is either experienced with actual death or threatened death. It could also be due to some serious injury, or it could be from sexual violence and these need to be experienced in one of four ways. It is obvious that something else called '*vicarious*' trauma is also part of the criteria although it has only been named since the latest manual came into being. It will be explained further later in this book.

We must seek to fulfil the criteria to establish the symptoms are definitely PTSD.

We need to measure if there is any intrusion symptoms present that are associated with the traumatic events that start after the event happened.

We need to measure any persistent avoidance after the event has occurred.

Then we need to measure alterations in cognitions and / or mood alterations, associated with the traumatic events and happening after the event.

We may see marked alterations in arousal and reactivity associated, and these may be beginning or get worse after the event.

Criteria urges that the duration of the symptoms continues for over one month.

We must clarify that the disturbances must cause clinically significant distress or impairment in social, occupational, or other important functioning in life.

Of course the disturbances must not be caused by substance abuse or prescriptions or any other medical condition that could cause complications or affect the diagnosis in any way.

We have also to be aware that some do not present with full criteria immediately and there may be a delay of some six months even though some symptoms were evident immediately after the event or within a month or more.

Criteria for children under six, is similar to adults but with specific differences due to their age and development which I will not go into here. Suffice it to say if there are any presenting issues or unusual behaviour or activity with children we should seek to examine their susceptibility that Trauma may have occurred.

The effects of trauma are so far reaching, in my opinion, that all issues of relational nature and aggressive behaviour and general withdrawal should be investigated thoroughly, before trying to engage in any other types of treatments, for anyone, especially young children.

Vulnerable children and adults are prime targets for 'trapped shock' and many are unable to hold or deal with these stressful events, children may also become stunted in development and possibly unable to talk properly, or even lose their speech completely. For example, one young girl living in Syria, sadly suffered mutism, at the age of 5, after her parents were tragically killed by the bombing.

Are diagnostic labels really helping?

I have a healthy network of well over 10,000 professional people currently on LinkedIn today, mainly Mental health Professionals and I find it's a constant source of interest and interchange of ideas. Other like-minded people are always sharing what turns their crank in the Mental Health arena about the numerous mental health developments and their critical evaluation of many things, which shows why it is a source of research interest, while being mildly entertaining with all the various arguments.

Why is it, universities do not make it a requirement, for student psychologists to have personal therapy? Maybe it would put them off studying at the University and stop the income to the Uni? It might justify the means for this outrageous lack of professional care for their students. This is huge!

While on Linked-In recently, I enjoyed a post, from a professional contact, quoting about psychiatric diagnosis concerns, like myself (I won't mention her name here) but this person wrote, in effect to say, '*she has gone away from the idea of "symptoms" and "illnesses"* and she had many supporters, whom agreed with her sentiments, myself included. So it appears many have come to similar conclusions about the DS-VM and the ICD-10, in that they are causing mental health sufferers, to be failed, by those who ought to be supporting them.

Without labels and medical jargon, we could help sufferers to cope better and probably to even survive some of the NHS treatment plans and even become healthier.

We agree with many others that unfortunately, and sadly we still need to maintain the current diagnostic criteria, at least for now, to enable sufferers to access social benefits and for other purposes, like legalities around insurance claims, courts, etc, as there is literally nothing else, at present to refer to, giving explanation that other professionals may follow effectually and officially.

We need to go back to the drawing board of diagnostic labels and see people and not projects and labels and the debate will go on until we reach a healthy conclusion, or not, of course.

What is the difference between PTSD and C-PTSD?

PTSD shortened from the words 'Post Traumatic Stress Disorder' is a mental health condition that can occur in people who have lived through a specific traumatic event or series of events that had a definitive time limit, or in many cases, only happen once.

We explain this type of PTSD as the **Stage 1** type of PTSD Trauma which is often, a single action Trauma, like an assault or single violent strike to the person, or a single act of rape, or a specific accident of some sort.

C-PTSD, shortened from the words 'Complex Post Traumatic

Stress Disorder' which is the result of prolonged exposure to trauma over long periods of time, often during childhood.

This we describe more fully as a **Stage 2** PTSD Trauma which is more about ongoing types of domestic violence, or sustained outside attacks, such as long term sexual abuse, or prolonged violence, or both, or in war zones and the extreme violence seen in veterans Trauma suffering long term combat stress, or with psychological mental manipulation as a form of abuse in different types of relationship dynamics within families or marriage.

When I am training potential counsellors in Convergence College, or even as a therapist using simple counselling techniques, or even when I am dealing with a more damaged client from a psychotherapeutic stance, we do tend to talk of our '**clients**'.

These clients are sometimes referred to by charitable organisations serving the general public, as 'service users', which makes me think of the term more humorously of these 'service users' whom at one time we would associate with those attending a public toilet at a train station or perhaps a drug addict seeking medical aid; yet this is the current trend of the politically correct brigade, so they are named as such in this generic term.

However, when dealing with Trauma with a capital '**T**', (in other words major **Trauma** in the present) and talking of the kind of Trauma we need to deal with straight away to give relief and that is full of symptoms, and destructive energy, which is in actual fact 'trapped shock'.

I would term Trauma sufferers as '**patients**' in this scenario, because we tend to give directives and give actual treatments and we also sometimes need to assist patients in a supportive physical way, by means of clinical touch for grounding, or by using a pointer physically and need to get very close to patients, for example, just like they do at the opticians and often working just a few inches in the front of the eyes, the same as nurses and doctors, and especially when we are using our Convergence

Eye Therapy (CET) using the latest intervention through deep relaxation and the Convergence By-Pass therapy (CBPT) Accessing the REM part of the brain and utilising the occipital nerves and Brain Re-Set procedures, using positive imagination and polyvagal theory as a direct intervention treatment, which is therefore necessarily carried out, on the clinical level in psychotherapies, though our treatments are completely without the need to prescribe the use of drugs.

Important - Sadness is not Trauma

Sadness is not necessarily Trauma, in the sense of PTSD, though sadness can be associated with Trauma as an affect held by a Trauma; such as when a person is traumatised by the physical damage witnessed to another or the death of a loved one, or the traumatic effect on a person simply witnessing another suddenly suffering from a terrible accident or someone dying tragically, or a sufferer being trapped with a horrifying image of that person's death.

I think of the nightly news report of the terrified young five year old girl who was suddenly struck dumb 'the effects of pure shock to her young mind', when she was faced with the horrific reality that she witnessed in seeing all her family being destroyed by bombs, in Syria. The brain is powerful and attempts to protect us from psychological damage and in this case shut down as it was too terrifying to even speak out her feelings or what she saw.

When we are describing stage 1 or stage 2 types of PTSD Trauma, we are certainly not referring to a simple traumatic episode that happened years ago when a family pet died and we were a little unhappy for a few days, but although it was probably quite serious for us and obviously somewhat traumatising in general terms, at the time, yet it had no lasting symptoms other than sad memories, which we all have to master in our lives. Life deals us certain cards and we have to live with sadness and loss where we need to go through a grieving process of change and find acceptance or we do not function well in this life. It is part of living after all.

It is quite strange how we have evolved in the West. As many will go to their GP when suffering simple sadness today, when a few nights rest and some proper sleep will no doubt work wonders for us (no wonder we all have issues today in getting to see the doctor) and these poor souls then get prescribed anti-depressants, when all they need to do is just allow themselves to feel these feelings and realise they are not going to die, or even get wounded beyond repair because (as we are often told) whatever does not kill you makes you stronger and as sad people, we will usually feel better in the morning after even one good night's sleep.

But we are so ingrained with the fact that we must alleviate any suffering at all and this means we should feel absolutely no pain whatsoever, then when we feel that sadness or upset, we immediately look to the doctor for what they may offer in biochemical relief (like others going to their drug dealers) and it's a wrong attitude, because it does not help us to be strong in the face of real pain and suffering. Sadness is part of living, so let people be sad (and by all means do cry with them) but don't shove pills down their throat to make everything better and teach them learned helplessness. We make a rod for our own back that way and do not grow to maturity.

Real Trauma with a capital 'T'

Real Trauma is different. I therefore have continued to write this Major impacting PTSD type of Trauma with a big 'T', as I call it, which is quite different from ordinary therapy.

Let me look at Trauma in a little more depth for the layman. I see Major Trauma being treated more from the 'clinical stance', in a closer hands-on work where we do actualise a different therapeutic alliance by bringing a healing treatment to psychological suffering through physical interventions, and using bodywork and sensory stimulations to facilitate change in the amygdala by Re-Setting the historic images in memory and alleviating and removing the corresponding shock, so in this sense of our engagement and the direct guidance and manipulations of the mind with our interactive therapy, which has nothing to do with the simple talking cure, or an amount of money exchanged.

Trauma therapy is, in the clinical sense, quite different from normal counselling skills in therapy; where we would normally allow the client to lead at their own pace such as in humanistic theory, following person centred theory to its logical end, where the patient is unable to lead. In Trauma we have to do the direct manipulation work for them and yet with them.

With Major Trauma it is very different within therapy in that we need to become more directive when the client allows so that we may deal more effectively in getting rid of the Major Trauma experienced. This may only be client led up to a point and then we need to guide the treatment more determinedly, in keeping the patient safe for example. Not to the point of being insensitive to a patient's needs of course, but quite directive in practice when moving a patient through the exercises to alleviate the Trauma(s).

Now talking about real Traumas, This is Traumatic Stress that is immediately quite debilitating and life changing in many ways, or has evolved into something severe after some time, which is almost unmanageable for the person suffering.

Post Traumatic Stress Disorder (PTSD)

I am talking here primarily about the fact that Trauma has become unmanageable and literarily turned into a 'disorder'. We have identified this, as something called Post Traumatic Stress Disorder, as described in the psychiatric diagnostic manuals in USA and Britain, or in laymen's terms we call it PTSD, as it is more commonly known today.

With PTSD we notice clusters of symptoms that are in the areas of Avoidance, Hyper-Arousal and Intrusivity, to the point of continually recurring causing constant disturbance and mental instability. This can certainly take over a person's life and cause a great deal of anxiety and mental pain which often disrupts sleep patterns, anxiety and depression which also affects normal family life.

Many turn to self-medication in some way, simply to try to distract themselves from the pain of raw memories and many find they experience triggers and events that bring the hurtful images or memories hurtling back into the mind, which causes major grief and disturbing feelings for the sufferer.

Complex PTSD

Complex PTSD, although all PTSD Trauma could be considered complex by those who don't really understand its true meaning in this respect. Note: More later under Trauma symptoms.

Vicarious Trauma

There is also another Trauma experience which is something we will discuss later and this is called 'Vicarious' Trauma which can be impacting on a 2nd person whom may be a separate party to the Trauma, or not even in the vicinity of the trauma or near victims of trauma, and is often associated with the discussions of the accounts of what has happened, or seeing the look on people's faces, or just overhearing conversations about traumas and/or hearing screams of the people caught in trauma or seeing videos or still photographs of events, such as 9/11 or reading reports, documentaries, animal fights, boxing, fighting of any type, etc. there are many different scenarios and effects when others are able to pick up the 'visuals' or 'imagined' feelings around these traumatic episodes.

The eyes have it – Vision (imagination) is key

In layman's terms I could best describe this type of Trauma event that we call 'Vicarious' trauma to think about, how we get quite 'spooked' at ghost stories, or horror movies, especially when we are younger. Some young children end up having nightmares for many years when they have seen something that they didn't understand that scared them.

Chucky and Freddie Kruger movies seen by young ones, when older children may have had access to the screen technology and play movies when there are no grown-ups around, to ask, what is currently being watched.

Unfortunately, their little girl or boy has wondered in and is watching fearfully from a distance perhaps, or when Mum or Dad has a babysitter who brings their own movie to watch and the children are allowed to sit up with them because the older baby sitter thinks it's only a film and if its just make believe, so surely it's not that bad, is it? Or worse when older kids or baby-sitters are watching hard-core porn and little impressionable eyes are not shielded from this adult material. Outcome trauma and some of it may become hidden for fear of repercussions if they were to snitch, or not being accepted and loved by their siblings if they spoil their fun or get them into trouble.

Teenagers too, have their own set of screamers and horror stories expressed in school around the mysterious and frightening images that could be in the mirrors and often taunted by older kids while at school.

Others can be freaked out by the words of others who threaten or bully them with words that conjure up all sorts of torture as a young adolescent. The imagination rules in the negative.

We humans can often get frightened about the unknown, which is primarily about the death instinct which comes to the fore when we don't know what will happen to us. I understand that we view parents through infantile eyes as gods and we discern that our fragile lives are in their hands. This then affects us greatly, imagine them fighting too.

This instinctual behaviour of self-preservation and resultant fear of annihilation when we become insecure, I believe, originates in our idealised parent interactions and as we witness them interacting with each other and more widely others later and with the world generally. We therefore get fearful and anxious and our imagination may completely run wild and cause all sorts of worry and sleeplessness and emotional upheaval and unconscious coping mechanisms.

When I am asked to see children who are anxious and depressed, some children attending are even considered suicidal; brought by their worried parents whom are struggling to make sense of what is going on with their usually buoyant child. This is more shocking to the parents when the child is apparently suddenly not coping well at school, or when the minor is away from home overnight which maybe at a school friend's or at the home of a separated parent or with their extended family.

I like to try to check out the concept of the death instinct and the child's undisclosed fears (away from Mum or dad – asking them to sit in ears length, just outside the door or partition) so that in more of a private conversation, other things come into light, and to see if there are any 'bogiemen' lurking in the shadow of their imagination, which may be playing havoc within the psyche, of the unfortunate and anxious minor.

Going back to the concept of Vicarious Trauma, it is my view that it is massively connected to the imagination and accesses the REM part of the brain even in our imagination and at the same time it is also connected to the occipital nerves (the nerves around the eyes) as in first hand Trauma and as it connects with the ANS (autonomic nervous system) routed through the Vagus nerve in polyvagal theory and further routes via the brainstem up to the prefrontal cortex and down to the eyes and at the same time is connected to the higher executive main cortex of the brain. We therefore access this Vicarious Trauma through both imagination and the occipital nerves in the same way as other Traumas in Convergence Psychotherapy.

And if we couple all that to the fact, which is well known within brief solution therapies, that the imagination either works positively for you, or negatively against you, then we may conclude that the Amygdala has through stimulation to the visual, or audio, coupled with kinaesthetic touch, or through imagined outer and inner feelings around the negative imagination of this new vision become stuck fast in fight, flight, or freeze mode and is therefore trapped in a dark negative part of the imagination where the Traumatic event(s) have a kind of frozen loop in the negative and the vicarious trauma loop is made complete. This is further amplified where the person is close to the traumatised person or involved deeply in hearing others express these feelings of horror or discomfort and pain. The vicarious trauma then finds a way through the imagination and emotional attachment to then cement the feelings, of empathic pain, as it attaches to the 2nd person or even third party interpersonal dynamic transfers are possible.

We also know through EMDR that much trauma is associated with the optical nerves and the position of the eyes when we take in trauma. We also know through David Grande's development of EMDR called Brainspotting that we can use the micro movements of the eye and the feedback of the patient to determine exactly where a memory is situated and find further detail to gain more clarity, which we use specifically at Convergence to locate blurred or hidden trauma.

This is born out experientially, when we often unconsciously move our eyes, to a certain place when we are trying to recall things from the past or when using our imagination to invent something. This is when we often move our eyes in order to access true historic memory or creative parts of the brain to facilitate the imagination, in other words, to make things up. This is often called 'Tells', where this knowledge is useful and may even help one determine if someone is lying to us, but only when we have previously logged their eye movements and scaled their interactions to see what areas are factual memory and what areas are imagined, even to order.

Many worry that taking a child or partner for Trauma therapy that they may become even more traumatised because they cannot think about the Trauma(s) let alone deal with them in therapy and talk about them.

The good news is this; one of the beauties of our treatments, is that for those sensitive narratives, we do not even need to know exactly what the Trauma is in detail to treat the Trauma effectively from the start. This is useful when there is so much shame around Trauma that emerges from a shameful experience, such as in childhood / adolescence sexual abuse.

Patients are safe with our expertise and will not be re-traumatised with our methods and treatments we use.

CHAPTER 3: TRUSTING PROFESSIONALS

There are those who eventually recognise and accept the effects of major Trauma in themselves, or pushed to get well, by family members, or well-meaning friends, so off they trot to their GP for some help, or are eventually referred by another practitioner for specialist help (realising as I write this that conservative British people have been programmed over decades to totally believe in what the Doctor says, or writes, if they can understand the GP's writing.

How can we question this ingrained infallibility of the GP, as some sort of perfect demigod who cannot possibly be wrong or God forbid if we think of dismissing the GP's trained diagnosis.

GP Guidance in Diagnosing PTSD

To diagnose post-traumatic stress disorder, your doctor will likely: Perform a physical exam to check for medical problems that may be causing your symptoms. Do a psychological evaluation that includes a discussion of your signs and symptoms and the event or events that led up to them.

Heavy Drugs for PTSD

Medications historically suggested to and prescribed by the GP's: In addition to sertraline and paroxetine, the SSRI fluoxetine has been recommended as first-line treatment (off label) for patients with PTSD. And If SSRIs are not tolerated, or are ineffective, SNRIs should be considered as a second-line treatment.

Therefore we act in trust regarding everything the Doctor tells us, or what they direct us to do, even to the point of giving us pills that may cause addictions like pain killers, or which may cause long term dependence, and the same with most anti-psychotics and anti-depressants, all of which are very powerful drugs indeed.

It is widely established in our profession that we need to be aware of re-traumatisation due to this proliferation of pills handed out as sweeties. We know that <u>Trauma may return, up to fifty percent</u> when a person suffering major Trauma is placed on anti-depressants or is on anti-psychotic medications and then is subsequently taken off of the strong pills after they have had their Trauma therapy.

Surely, it would be infinitely better, to get the patient to the therapist faster and then there is no need for the pills in the first place, but Oh! No, that is not the way it works. Obviously some need the drugs to survive ordeals, but with proper Trauma therapy, they would not need it.

Case in point. I was informed recently that a patient has been going to therapy for three years and the person is still having PTSD symptoms and the advanced counsellor, although having managed to reduce severity of some lessor symptoms, unfortunately had not been able to shift the real PTSD Trauma symptoms! How unsurprising is that? based on what we know of outdated trauma training, or the latest grossly ineffective bolt on style trauma informed therapy (obviously this is cheaper in training lesser qualified staff) which is being rolled out to be used in the referrals either from doctors surgeries (who are also not informed or skilled widely enough in mental health) or it is simply pedalled through the hospitals as a cheap alleged remedy to ease the suffering, but it does not cure it.

Not everyone is in it for the money, but three years for the person undergoing trauma treatment regarding a Trauma that has not been resolved to date, would be considered by many opportunists counsellors, as good money if you could get it, so please beware that there are unscrupulous people, even in the professions who are continuing to bleed people with no established results and this is not helping our cause, which is to get these poor suffering people real and immediate help and support that delivers fast.

Counsellors need to realise that PTSD sufferer's families, particularly the spouses and their children do not have the time to mess around, once this family time has gone, it has gone forever, its gone, so they really should not have to wait for proper specialised treatment!

One wonders why the young 17 year old girl in the headlines recently, sought euthanasia and who allegedly suffered from the Trauma of sexual abuse and reported in the media.

This all begs the question, why was this young woman not sign-posted and encouraged strenuously, by those friends around her, or her GP and any other counsellors, teachers, or other carers?; What real help was she offered, that would have been extremely helpful to stop her early Traumas around abuse?

The solemn fact that she felt the need to talk seriously to a Dutch Euthanasia clinic and sadly choosing to die, instead of finding modern effective Trauma therapy that could have really changed her life. We are left with a felt sense of what a terrible waste of a young life.

If this young woman was talking about her Trauma(s) openly to the someone surely there is a need to make other professionals aware and bring this into the public domain more.

But without labouring the point too much, what a crying shame to hear of this tragedy of a human being's death, when it could so easily have meant healing and life for this young adult. We must make it a priority for all carers to become aware of the latest Trauma help available to all sufferers. What a strange position we find ourselves in today with actions of this kind going on. It makes little sense why Trauma therapy is not being advertised and highlighted in the media more on what help there is out there, rather than perpetuating these tragedies and continuing to hear these terrible stories of people suffering without finding relief.

As an admired national newspaper columnist, Richard Littlejohn, also the author of 'Littlejohn's Britain', is an amazing writer and humorously draws attention to the crazy political correctness and the hypocrisy seen in society and unbalanced and unhealthy values especially regarding expressions of distorted morality from many public figures and the job's worth public servants within the authorities in this land, when he writes of all the stupid nonsense and extremes that politicians and crusaders of their truths and those in authority actually go to, and what nonsensical statements they come up with today in UK. He often sartorially states, at the end of his commenting, *"You couldn't make it up!"* – I wholeheartedly agree with this sentiment, which in our case relates primarily to the attitude to of mental health care in this country. It is so ludicrous, you couldn't make it up! Well could you?

But what about those who come to, what they believe is, fairly normal counselling help, probably attending due to issues in their families or workplace issues or other situations where they may have overreacted or could not cope or have severe anxieties or destructive panic attacks, or other situations that they feel uncomfortable about and where they cannot seem to get back up after being knocked down by life's knocks. Usually they come because they are not coping with life and all its ups and downs and in some situations this behaviour is fuelled by trauma of some sort.

I believe that carers need to see how important it is to look for the signs of Trauma too, as many are often unaware of Trauma in everyday life. Many within the caring professions miss the signs and do not suspect Trauma due to lack of training or awareness, let alone suggest it for further exploration, so its important to realise the reluctance to consider or even refer someone who may be suffering Trauma to a specialist, just like some do not see the signs of Autism, which could also be quite aggravated by Trauma, for many and varied reasons.

I personally have heard very different misdiagnoses and excuses and labelled incorrectly within medical care, and/or counselling, where carers qualified in respectable training institutions, supposedly have been trained for excellent service to the general public. One must question this lack of awareness in the professions and a cavalier attitude to Trauma and ask why carers are not being fully prepared to see these obvious signs of these two major traits of Trauma and those of ASD?

Excuses like these are given regularly:

This is what I hear as excuses, often with student placements seen in supervision. Things like, I don't feel qualified to identify it in my clients (or patients). I didn't realise there was trapped shock in this person. It seemed like a fairly normal situation that the client had been through, but they did not seem to respond to normal counselling help (but no idea it may be Trauma!). CBT didn't seem to help this person. They were too frightened to get help about that. I was trained as a counsellor / therapist that shock would just need to be dealt with' overtime' which heals and normal counselling would allow the trauma to gradually heal. NO!, NO!, NO! please reconsider the approach. Ask?

Ok, so there is a get out clause from the institutions, like the one I was trained in that said; "This is a very specialised area and although the NHS offer CBT it is still a specialised area so better to leave it alone for now".

And this; "Oh, you cannot get involved until you have been a psychotherapist for at least 5 years and then you may start training in something called EMDR, which is very expensive. I was also told this by a tutor while in supervision:

"For extreme cases patients sometimes have to be hospitalised and injected / medicated, while the trauma work is carried out, as they get re-traumatised with this method of EMDR up to 80% of the original

trauma and in that scenario could die of a heart attack at that time, as the trauma therapy is fierce, and could re-traumatise the patient or there could be a serious abreactions taking place, who knows?".

In some part I need to agree this may be true, but it also was designed to frighten the life out of the majority of the students on my course when they heard this. Obviously it's not good for those who do not understand enough to be dabbling in Trauma work.

We tell all of our students that *"Some techniques we use in major Trauma therapy at tier-one can be really quite simple and easy to teach, but seriously not to be used as a party trick".* Hence the confidential reciprocity in our work with patients.

Unfortunately, there was one student who reported she had been to a party and acted out what she had gleaned from some Trauma therapy with another friend and fortunately nobody was hurt in the process, as she remembered to do the right thing, at the time, but it could have been catastrophic, she was truly reprimanded of course. This is never to be carried out in a social setting particularly around those who are drunk enough to risk mental health and who may go and try this at home with disastrous consequences.

I tell all my patients this is very 'confidential' material and not even to try to explain what I do or show them, to others, regarding what is done in therapy, other than this simple statement, to close off the local gossip's curiosity:-

"I signed a legal confidentiality contract, which states, I can't tell you what the specialist did, because it is dangerous to try it outside, and I could be liable for any damage caused by anyone I tell who may attempt untrained therapy, but it worked for me".

The problem is this, some students attending personal therapy (because of diploma requirements) have been trained in certain elements of this trauma work at a low level within psychotherapy training and therefore experienced some of the initial simple techniques in training, or in their personal therapy requirements when attending one of our own College trained graduate psychotherapists, and these techniques are incredibly useful in the right hands, to deal with many life issues, but could still prove problematic when these techniques are ignorantly trotted out.

The therapy offered in my time, post training, originally was basically simple Cognitive Behaviour Therapy, until recently, when it was upgraded and called 'trauma focused Cognitive Behaviour Therapy' (or 'tf CBT' for short). Remember that it is infinitely cheaper than the more specialised forms of treatment offered by the independent practitioners so that is why many g to the GP in the first place to get the free treatment even if it lets them down long term. More recently the NHS uses specialists trained in Eye Movement Desensitisation and Reprocessing, (EMDR) for short, that is used for severe cases.

CBT, EMDR - Mainline NHS Treatments for Trauma

EMDR is an individual therapy and typically delivered one to two times per week, for a total of 6-12 sessions, although it is reported that some people benefit from fewer sessions (this is

relevant to 'one-off' Traumas or lower impact trauma stress).

Sessions can be conducted on consecutive days, (although we believe this is far too harsh and is often quite stressful and causes very high anxiety with no time to recuperate, when delivered as twice per weekly sessions, there surely needs to be time in between to reduce internal stressors).

EMDR is now being used in different therapeutic situations. EMDR is an eight-phase treatment method. (1) History taking. (2) client preparation. (3) assessment. (4) desensitization. (5) installation. (6) body scan. (7) closure and (8) re-evaluation of the treatment. These are the eight phases of this treatment, briefly described.

Just today, I was talking to a patient who suffered actual torture at the hands of evil people and needing help and was given a useless treatment plan, of so called bespoke therapy for Complex

PTSD, which primarily consisted, of him being told to go home and try to relax and the treatment? This involved smelling perfume, or thinking of happy thoughts, or concentrating on being mindful, or by simply concentrating on any good times of the past and that was supposed to help heal him. Surprise! none of which, even reduced, or touched his Trauma shock. You just couldn't make it up!

But he was told that specialist treatment would be a long time coming and there were no referrals being made at that time because of the waiting times and the lack of resources.

But nobody suggested to this poor man, until I spoke with him that there was hope. That he could be freed from this suffering and ongoing torture, by a specialist psychotraumatologist, even though it would mean 'going private' to remove the trauma instead of simply trying to reduce anxiety a little around the Trauma, but it was going to resolve the problem by investing in himself and particularly his future, using a Trauma specialist. He would have jumped at the chance to do that to find relief from his nightmare.

The DSVM-5 (the latest psychiatric manual of mental health disorders) also is unhelpful to relieve immediate suffering because with this latest diagnostic criteria which states patients suffering PTSD (Post Traumatic Stress Disorder) requires those overwhelming symptoms have to be constant, for at least four weeks, to determine the trauma symptoms have continued after that time, so clinicians may then officially label the suffering as PTSD, then we may confirm it shows the correct 'dubious' criteria, to be named after all, as full blown PTSD.

If you are suffering greatly from all these symptoms, which are sometimes scaled from very raw, to fierce, to completely debilitating, how helpless and uncared for, would that leave you feeling by any therapist or clinician, before being allowed proper specialist psychological Trauma treatment, surely you would question their concerns for your wellbeing, or what empathy they had?

Just for a moment, consider what that may be like for an extremely traumatised patient, to just be told (by a supposedly caring therapist) you need to wait and endure these frightening symptoms and often terrifying and extremely disturbing feelings and just to see what happens? It would be like being in terrible pain of diagnosed appendicitis or maybe a duodenal ulcer and to be told to take an aspirin and go home and wait to see if it gets worse and then we will treat you. Only then, once you have suffered more and you even go into physical shock, will we confirm the diagnosis to your problem and give you some specialist treatment relief!

Are we seriously expected to behave that way when we know through experience that we have the ability to resolve these Traumas fast and yet we are supposed to wait for a month and see? It's utter nonsense really! But for the sake of court actions or tribunals, we are supposed to take this line of action. Really? It's barbaric, even to suggest it to a thoroughly caring professional, who has all the means at their disposal to alleviate a Trauma patient's suffering, right from the get go.

I am not prepared to wait to offer relief, even though the NHS Mental health staff with their psychiatric labels, need that time to deliberate to function in determinations or actions, this situation has obviously rippled out to occupational health (eap's) rehab organisations, and insurance companies, of course.

Obviously in this world of monetary rules and regulations the official medical officers in authority when referring someone for PTSD therapy needs to be covered adequately by referencing labels and to ensure the patient is documented according to the right of passage in the mental health Conveyor Belt System and thereby qualify for funding. Unfortunately things often come down to money.

I think also of the forces Veterans we see each year around remembrance day, whom at the age of 80's and 90's are still on overwhelm 75+ years later and still suffering the effects of war violence and Traumatisation when they could get help and who will lead them to be treated so they no longer suffer? What are GP' doing in their surgeries when veterans come in? They could ask the three important questions on our section here on identifying Trauma. Just the three questions inform us all.

I also think of those who have suffered Trauma in the now and what is going on with the work related eap's and insurance companies backing the inadequate treatment plans being put forward.

How often have I been asked to perform simple CBT counselling only to find out a person is suffering Trauma when they have apparently had telephone interview assessments prior to attending my therapy with a list of symptoms as long as your arm and anxious to the point of suicide ideation.

They have these jobs to assess, but lack the in depth training. No mention of Trauma therapy required though, one such person got annoyed with me and decided to place the patient elsewhere because I said they do not need counselling they need Trauma specialisation, but that didn't fit their quota allotted to this client! Hmm, so it is again because it costs more money to offer these poor unfortunate souls the real help they so desperately need.

I think of the Her Majesty's Prison Service, as one example of cost cutting, by their security service and the occupational health offering for the staff of that company who were cutting back so much, that they put their wardens at risk. Expecting Prison Wardens to go in to sort out violent fights, (whilst a peer or manager was busy) and where the individual could be facing sometimes, upwards of twenty young men on their own, is it any surprise that the Wardens I saw for therapy, eventually had been taken hostage, or badly beaten by inmates, whilst at work and at some point Traumatised and developed PTSD, where they could not do their job until they had Trauma therapy.

Though this was not fully recognised by those who were assessing them and even suggestions that this was only a bit of a traumatic event, or one suggested it's just Post Traumatic Stress and not PTSD. Strangely enough, I was requested over the telephone to only to give these people six weeks counselling, with CBT being the operative therapy offering and if they needed a bit more, to come back to ask the occupational employment organisation (eap) and told by them, we may be able to offer a further six weeks, if the employer agrees. Really!

Once, I explained it was specialist Trauma therapy required and we needed to increase the funding and although they offered more for a short while, nevertheless the contract eventually went elsewhere, no doubt to a somewhat more compliant therapist. Sad, after I voiced my opinions about the incorrect diagnosis and made up assessments, without the eap clinicans recognising the reality of Trauma, that I instantly recognised, they soon replaced me with other counsellors, who would offer to 'reduce their suffering a little, for less pament'. At the same time, not to make waves and no doubt keep their mouths shut and work for lower, but regular fees, which kept the ball rolling and the abuses continuing. My conscience, as a professional wounded healer, does not let me do that. You couldn't make it up!

CHAPTER 4: LOOKING FOR SYMPTOMS

If you are a counsellor or therapist you need to understand what to look for. Symptoms in general follow a pattern.

It must be 'TRAUMA FIRST'

Because I have seen so many stuck clients and stuck patients walk into our offices and confess they have had counselling / therapy before and when assessed, it is fairly evident (usually with much overwhelm present) that there is evidence of previous Trauma(s), which is holding up the flow of normal feelings such as grieving or anger management and normalised coping skills and at the same time probably holding up therapy interventions and therefore, no doubt, blocking the healthy improvement of the patient presenting in therapy, so we ask the three questions (to follow) that matter in identifying real Trauma.

Surely, as a duty of care, we must start to recognise these traumatic events and look for hidden Trauma too. It is certainly always better to err on the side of caution, when offering a diagnosis on something we know little about, but that lack of knowledge in this area can be the means to block a patient from recovery, from any mental health problem, or emotional issues.

We are now much more informed, through the interchange of modern ideas on the internet and the whistle-blowers, just how carelessly mental health psychiatrists, or clinical psychologists, have wrongly labelled patients, declared to be borderline, bi-polar, or suffering a form of psychosis, and even missing the relevance of the way Trauma has an affect generally and/or, on Autistic patients.

Therefore counsellors and all professionals need to be more aware now and ready to identify the symptoms preventing short term improvements, or a return to a healthier state, by seeing the log jams in the river of mentally damaged people coming through our doors seeking help. My vision for these types of patients with Trauma looks like this.

Each one comes in with all manner of problems they want us to solve, and Trauma clients are carrying a vast dam of healing potential, which is dragged behind them and simply wasting and putrefying, simply because few nurses, doctors, or counsellors and even therapists, are opening their eyes to see the log jam of Trauma holding everything good and normal back. So if we were to see the Trauma we could remove the log jams and get the river flowing again. Mental health at last. So we need to say to ourselves, it has to be TRAUMA FIRST!!

The 3 easy questions GP's need to ask patients

Three questions that help any GP's, Nurses, or clinical / medical carers, in diagnosing possible PTSD, it is important to see the signs, when the patient has presenting issues, around anxiety, excessive worrying, nervousness, depression, psychosis, or with people labelled as having a personality disorder, particularly the latest trend of non-specific personality disorder, bypolar, addictive behaviours, etc.

"Did anything else happen around the time the symptom(s) first occurred?"

Although at first, this seems so obvious, yet it's surprising how often it gets missed by professionals. "I wonder, how long you have lived with these life restricting problems?". Then leading to the next question...

"Is it still upsetting to talk about it?"

This is such an important part of assessing whether a particular memory needs de-Traumatising.

My follow up to clarify to the patient, is this,

"I wonder, if this still feels as raw and painful today, when you think of it?"

When we ask, we often see the signs of the patient, welling-up (overwhelm) and maybe a lump in the throat, and where tears appear the patient is beginning to show a little disturbance. Maybe mentioning or remembering the event is a bit painful

"I wonder, if this makes you almost as upset, as it did at the time".

It sounds obvious, but the quickest way to find out whether you need to treat Trauma, is simply to clarify

"Does it hurt now, when you go there in your mind?" And this is the last confirmation to refer on to Trauma work...

"Is the memory trapped?"

PTSD types - Traumatic memories, because of how (it is thought) they become trapped (looping) somewhere between the amygdala (the involvement of the fight, flight, or freeze, part of the brain) and the hippocampus which calms the reactions (an area where recent memories are stored) and unfortunately these Trauma memories do not fade with time, like normal memories, because they are literally hot-wired (contained) in that part, of the mind, brain, continuum, causing mayhem for the sufferer.

Neutral, or pleasant memories, start to disappear and feel that they were experienced quite a long time ago, as they become stored in the neocortex and begin to blur a little. Yet persistent traumatic memories, as in PTSD - unresolved Trauma, don't get transferred into long term memory, and they are quite vivid memories, unless we help these poor patients to do that, which will only recover healthier thought processing again through specialist Psycho-Trauma work.

This should help to release more patients from the standard CBT route, to find true relief from Trauma by finding a specialist treatments service that remove Trauma and not just help the sufferer a little or even a lot, it needs to be removed fully, so they may live more healthily.

I have worked with many traumatised people, some of whom had traumas stretching back a long way. Yet these types of memories, all felt very recent, or seemed energised currently, no matter how long ago the trauma was experienced.

When a patient is suffering any symptoms associated with Trauma we need to check it out and the pain could be eased much faster than carrying on with long term, time healing therapy or CBT. But sadly there is the rub, although ethically, all counsellors know we must not keep clients coming to us simply for the money, but when counsellors 'need' clients, such as on student placement to qualify, mainly due to their college requirements, or when it is to do with those running counselling businesses, where they need to pay their own expenses, it is no surprise in this economy, that client ethics can be overridden here, by the simple need to retain a paying client, as it represents income they all need to survive.

Beware counsellors keeping you in sessions when there is nothing happening in the long term, especially when it comes to suspected Trauma problems. However we do know some clients are quite resistant (unconsciously) to therapy and can waste their own time and money, by not cooperating properly, or simply being unable to access emotions, or memories easily and may need much more time, you cannot force in that situation, only continue to encourage movement forward.

Because of this, we explain further to our students on placement, and again remind them after graduation, that if they realise their client is suffering from Trauma, they need to refer to our specialists for Trauma work but we will ensure that the client they sent to us is sent straight back to them immediately after the therapy work has been done, alternatively we will find them another client to replace the one they sent us. This solves the problem of holding onto clients.

The Trauma work, which often may only last a couple of sessions to remove it from the place of trapped shock into the normal cortex and memory cells in the brain, mainly if the client has suffered only one main trauma, such as a rape, or an accident, or an act of violence, which becomes immediately evident, but obviously it is not so quick with complex trauma though. But again they will not usually lose, because we will always send the student a client in return for their referral.

These are some of the signs you may find in your work.

You may have wondered in the past, when seeing people in therapy, why some service users are on overwhelm whenever the subject of any particular hurts are opened, or if they are stuck in a particular situation, that you have been attempting to deal with, in counselling and where the client cannot seem to move forward emotionally and affect change.

Or when we are working with those, who have not been able to work, through situations, like a person typically grieving and continuing with bereavement counselling. Some may have attended with a competent bereavement counsellor for many sessions.

Kate

I had one such patient we shall call Kate, a middle aged, overweight woman, with children, who found she was always waking up in the middle of the night because she was fearful of having a heart attack in her sleep, which is how her mother had died when she was young. She never dealt with the weight issue and that was obviously also playing on her mind too and she had been on all the diets, although she had ben to more than one counsellor she could not gain peace and missed her mother a great deal.

This pointed me to a possible early trauma and one that had not been resolved because her counsellor did not have the experience to either identify possible trauma or be prepared to accept limitations of the counsellor and refer up so that any psychological block could be dealt with because without the trauma removed this client was not going to get past this block to get her life back.

Once we dealt with the trauma she moved on and began to improve and within a few more sessions the healing took place.

Or it could be someone in relational work, with a partner, or it could be regarding sex itself and specifically sexual parameters where a trauma has affected a client quite badly and the client is unable to get past it to relax in a marriage or other relatively long term relationship, the client sometimes does not know why they are feeling unable to settle with a partner and they think it has something to do with earlier sexual issues, but they don't have a problem with sex itself, but rather, the trust issues, for example, when around a new a partner and other sexuality issues, like shame or guilt.

However let us look now at the major Trauma symptoms in more detail.

TRAUMA PTSD can affect people regardless of age, race, gender — or even veteran status. It's important to know the signs and symptoms so we can direct people to the support they need.

First the Symptoms of PTSD

Whilst we do not agree with the way the DSM has been developed, nevertheless this is the current standard we all used, though I can foresee that may well change in the future.

However, in my view, an essential feature of Major Trauma 'PTSD' is the developing symptoms directly related to the traumatic experience.

Though it's not necessary for a person with PTSD to exhibit every symptom I am outlining, yet these are the most common areas of affect, showing PTSD symptoms.

We usually ask the patient to fill in an 'Impact of Events' form, to enable us to attempt at scaling the Trauma impact on their lives, at that current moment.

We look at Avoidance, Intrusion and Hyper-Arousal in particular.

(1). The Symptom of Intrusion

A person with PTSD often experiences intrusive symptoms of the traumatic event in a number of ways including:

There are Recurring involuntary and distressing memories of the traumatic event

You will notice Recurring dreams or nightmares

There can also be Dissociative reactions and/or flashbacks

A patient experiencing these types of symptoms may also experience severe emotional distress, or physiological responses, like sweating, or trembling, or even feeling feint, in a situation that may remind them of this Trauma. They may even feel pains and have belly aches or headaches and develop other psychosomatic illnesses if the Trauma is not dealt with.

And we also see in children play times, with their themes in play, of the events in the trauma(s) coming through, and it is interesting to see how they may be expressed, without the child even realising this.

(2). The Symptom of Avoidance

The attitude of Avoidance can be a common symptom in other mental illnesses of course, such as social anxiety, an avoidant personality disorder and obsessive-compulsive disorder (OCD) throws this one up too.

For people with signs of PTSD though, avoidance can be both external and internal and primarily emotional. There are a couple of ways avoidance commonly shows up with people that have PTSD:

There is an External avoidance: where they avoid certain people, places, activities and objects that are reminders of the traumatizing event, this could be work or anything.

Then there is an Internal avoidance: the emotions cannot take the pressure the feelings bring up so they supress and avoid even thinking about, they will usually keep deflecting off and the patient may get quite angry with anyone, if they were to push it in any way, they do not want to remember, or discuss the traumatic event with anyone.

As an example a person who has survived an accident perhaps the victim of a an event like watching people being hurt or being hurt themselves and may begin to externally avoid an area perhaps by going out of their way to avoid the place where the accident occurred, even if that means taking a longer route.

Another example of emotional avoidance is where an ex-forces hero, just cannot deal with the issues surrounding their time in service abroad and are also unable to disclose to their family any details of the traumatic events of war, because they just don't need to think about it at all.

(3). Then there is the Symptom of Hyper-Arousal

Some feel this is a bit like that seen in a child who has been beaten and has been around a violent character like a father with anger issues.

PTSD sufferers often experience these types of symptoms, such as a hyper-vigilance, which is a heightened awareness and alertness, these are often easily frightened and startle easily which has an accompanying irritability and angry reactions ensue.

There may be a reckless or destructive behaviour setting in, which is quite cavalier in essence, where they will often go absent, almost a running away from responsibilities (which is often out of character) they may self-medicate and get drunk and take risks, not normally taken.

They may also have great difficulty concentrating and sleeping becomes an issue, often only managing a few hours sleep each night and have feelings of exhaustion when the Trauma really bites.

As our patients find incredible relief, almost immediately, as we begin to take the tops off of the mountains of their Trauma energy and pain, we notice as the shock is removed, how often this tiredness shows up.

Because the sufferers have been holding on so tight, to stop themselves going into melt down, the exhaustion usually shows itself, when the patient begins to feel more relaxed after their therapy and then starts yawning, which causes them to recognise and admit just how tired they were feeling at last. It proves they were really struggling to hold on!

There is also accompanying trust issues with PTSD and the sufferer has struggled with self-esteem issues and lack of confidence, as well as extreme feelings of guilt and/or shame.

But the hyper-arousal in these cases is usually more specific. It is more about the proneness to specific noises, as triggers, or with triggers by sounds, or smells, and may be certain looks or actions seen in others.

(4). Negativity and depression, or even dissociation

For people with PTSD, thinking and mood changes can affect the ability to form and maintain close friendships or relationships. The person becomes withdrawn and yet can become a party animal on the surface but withdrawing quite fast from social events.

Those with PTSD may also struggle with emotional numbness and feel hopeless about the future. Some other changes may occur at the same time.

(5). You may see changes in a person's mood / thinking

There will sometimes be persistent negative beliefs about oneself, or a person's situation. Maybe thinking that "I must be bad", or that "You can't trust people" these are quite strong examples.

There are feelings of being 'detached' from others, along with the thousand mile stare that is commonly found in Trauma sufferers.

You will notice a lack of any interest in those once enjoyed activities prior to the Trauma period.

Then you may notice the person has an inability to experience positive emotions like happiness or loving feelings which continue.

Because of sleep hygiene there is the Memory or cognition problems developing.

What we can see in Traumatised patients is a symptom many patients suffer is the belief that it is their fault. That they are somehow responsible which is hard to comprehend in certain situations. However, these thoughts are real and we must validate them, but it leads patients to push others away at times and may lead to loneliness and problem behaviour patterns, which we need to address.

Trauma Patient Philosophy (TPP)

We call this the Trauma Patient Philosophy (TPP) and there is a great deal of research right now on the way this TPP changes, after effective and life changing Trauma therapy. Where the person's view and corresponding philosophy of life begins to change, especially in relation to love, trust and relationships.

When a person suffers major Trauma, particularly with Complex Trauma, or protracted Traumatising events, the patients philosophy changes in relation to trust and 'trusting' of others becomes an issue.

Therefore the Trauma sufferer finds difficulty in relationship(s) and finding a balance around the whole arena of love and personal boundaries, this is often where misdiagnosis begins to take place from the acting out and frequently wrecked relationships.

In my view, for some sufferers of child abuse, for example, promiscuity may come in to being, from a position of desperation. Through Trauma abuse and confused feelings and anxieties, their quest to find real love and then not trusting in recognising, or finding it is thwarted. In this case, often not knowing the difference between, mature love and sexual attraction, the person often breaks already fragile relationships, by the sufferer perhaps holding on too tightly and becoming obsessive, or trying to control their potential partner, and usually self-sabotaging their early relational opportunities.

For some, it has become almost a revolving door of sexual partners, which is often emotionally draining and possibly damaging for their children too. In my mind, this is all too often misdiagnosed and associated with borderline personality disorder, especially when coupled with short periods of psychosis, instead of recognising Trauma induced behaviours.

Alternatively, if at an early age the person was taught strict sexual boundaries with an iron fist, or with very strong authoritarian words promoting a need to fear anything of a bodily or sexual nature, or where they were totally restricted from seeing other infants without clothes.

This could possibly have been coupled with attempts in sexual advances, that were recognised at an early age, even in play, or if an adult was frighteningly involved, in trying to sexualise that patient, which could be enough to Traumatise a child, quite early on, in life.

The Trauma would come, in some cases, because there had been a complete mystery built up around the portrayed 'evils of sex' and differences in sexuality, or in some cases their Trauma was due to abusive or violent sexual encounters, which may have frightened the sufferer away from a natural sexuality, by that I mean, in terms of procreation, namely designed between a man and a woman, this sufferer may possibly prefer to settle for an abstinence, quite understandably, from a position of fear.

But in some cases, for example, and I am convinced by client feedback, that some women have decided to seek alternate lifestyles, not because they were necessarily gay, but at times certain women have come from a position of fear, that terrifying potential for violence, or fear experienced in abusive past relationships, or simply where the past experiences of being controlled, or perhaps a terrorised childhood causing confused internal contact and distorted dialogues, where the sufferer seeks to find solace and gentleness in another caring woman. This has historic support form those who have testified to this dynamic of fear and sexuality. In reality although some women have covered their fear, by saying they are not interested in men, there are still some who, in reality, are still actually physically attracted to men and not to women, but through fear, deliberately will not allow themselves to go there.

However, for some it is also an excuse to explore their modern view of sexuality and it may satisfy a pure lust. Some women do become, or because it is now fashionable, have chosen to be bisexual too. This is not to suggest I am making any moral judgements, or saying lesbian women should go back to being with men, that is their own issues and decision, not mine.

What I am merely explaining, is from a psychotherapy reality, to be considered, around certain Trauma affect, in relation to the fears and the mistrust position of some sufferers. We are now going to look more deeply at the signs around Complex Trauma.

Complex Post Traumatic Stress Disorder

We know that many patients with **Complex Post Traumatic Stress Disorder** (called **C-PTSD** for short) may experience symptoms that are similar to the recognised and typical PTSD, but we must realise that the treatment may not be quite as straightforward as when we deal with regular PTSD.

Why is this? Because when we compare the complex nature of issues around C-PTSD to the regular PTSD, we notice that C-PTSD involves a much deeper wound to the psyche, which makes the symptoms of complex PTSD even more difficult to work with in therapy.

CHAPTER 5: SIGNS & SYMPTOMS

Let us now look at some of the common signals of Complex Post Traumatic Stress Disorder now abbreviated as C-PTSD:

Many symptoms are the same as PTSD. There are usually Flashbacks (often emotional flashbacks). Nightmares – often interrupting sleep hygiene. Difficulty maintaining close and trusting relationships with others. There is usually a sense of heightened irritability. Memory issues can be a problem too (this often blocks out reminders of the Trauma events). Usually there are severe feelings of guilt and shame involved. There is a marked decrease in interest with previously enjoyable activities.

Dissociation issues

Sometimes there is a noticeable element of dissociation, often witnessed by close relatives, or partners, which can be like a 'phasing out' or 'trance state' and can also be noticed where the sufferer notices body parts becoming elongated, or finding a sense of looking down upon oneself, or out of body experience, maybe a feeling of being disconnected from their body, not remembering where they have been walking or driving, etc.

One such client Robin, as an example, said he would often feel very light and see himself floating above the bed, as though he were looking down at himself, while he was in bed with his wife, whom he loved, as he was making love (we joked, at having a different sensation, than a romantic notion, 'as feeling the earth move') and at other times he reported, that he would often feel strange sensation, while he was driving, feeling that his arms and legs became elongated, just like 'Bananaman' and it's as if he was sitting on the back seat, but still driving along holding the wheel and operating the pedals. Many other people seem to phase out, while driving longer distances on the Motorways, and often when it is their well-travelled routes, can't recall much of the journey at all.

One of the most difficult symptoms that many people with C-PTSD face is the belief that they are personally responsible for any of the Trauma(s) that may have happened to them.

These are completely 'no-win' cycles of intrusive thoughts and they quite often lead to the sufferer pushing other people away, or maybe where the person becomes isolated and lonely, it can also lead to unhelpful and self-destructive patterns of thought and the onset of distracting behaviours and eventually tends to develop into profound interpersonal difficulties. This starts as a spiritual reality to do with their faith and by that, I mean their soul trust. The way they manifest in the world is somewhat distorted, in that they do not manifest well, they are troubled souls and have difficulty relating to the world and to people generally in various relationships.

Toxic Shame

Something else comes into this arena, which is termed Toxic Shame and is a common issue survivors of complex trauma endure. John Bradshaw remarks on Toxic Shame, highlighted with a poem '*My Name Is Toxic Shame*', in his book '*Homecoming*', which I must encourage, as an essential read. According to John, he used some words from a powerful meditation of *Leo Booth's*. and he also reworked this poem from some of his earlier exploration work on toxic shame from, '*Bradshaw on Healing the Shame That Binds You*'.

We know that Toxic Shame is something very raw, worse than guilt, the common feelings deep inside, of being faulty goods, or never coming up to the grade, or never being good enough. Whereas, if you are actually guilty of doing something wrong there is hope, because you can do something about that, possibly even repair it and make amends somehow. But with toxic shame, there is nothing that you could possibly do to resolve it. These feelings are usually at the central system of our less than feelings determined often by the introjected Lifescript of each person. This is what is at the heart of our core beliefs, about our personhood, and effects our very being and the way we manifest within this world.

Often the abusers will make a survivor feel that they deserved the treatment or the abusers form of love, or the survivor was the reason for it. Therefore we notice, often the survivors will be made to feel they don't deserve to be treated in any other way.

When we consider sexual abuse it shows there can be a whole new added layer of toxic shame created, and which needs a particularly specific and compassionate therapy, to help the survivor allow this to become accessible.

It is usual for those suffering sexual abuse and who are or have been repeatedly enduring this terrible abuse may develop feelings of being dirty, rubbish, or damaged and disgusting specifically when their bodies are violated in this distorted and intimately sexual intrusion.

There is a sense of being quite helpless. The survivor can develop a sense of hopelessness — that nothing will ever be the same and / or even OK. This is due to enduring the ongoing or repeated abuse. The survivor may feel so utterly damaged, that the person can see no hope for anything to get better again. As the person is faced with long periods of abuse, it can feel like there is no hope of anything changing in the foreseeable future, so there is no hope. Scriptures say "without vision the people die". Roughly translated, in Booty's Notes, format, this means 'without hope, life is surely without purpose and meaningless, where all future life seems to be bleak.

When the abuse stops, it does not mean the Trauma stops, so the survivor can continue having these very deep feelings at core belief level where they simply act in hopeless aimless lifestyles. At the same time there is this intensified and the life-threatening symptoms that occur around Complex PTSD. This keeps the sufferer stuck in the Trauma, with little hope of this easing.

This Manifests More as a Deep Fear to Trust

This is likely to be prevalent more in the sufferers who may endure ongoing abuse, just like those who may have suffered at the hands of a paedophile ring, or in child sex trafficking, or particularly sufferers abused regularly by trusted friends, or anyone admired around the family, or in their neighbourhood, or at school, because this protracted abuse obviously causes a deep fear of trusting people generally.

What happens when the abuse was by parents or caregivers, it makes the suffering greater so this fear and mistrust intensifies. This ongoing trauma re-wires the brain for fear and distrust. It is the way the brain develops to cope with any more intrusive potential abuse.

Complex Trauma sets people up to fail. The survivors often find trusting anyone (especially what they considered at first a distant God who failed them, instead of the loving God who wants to restore them and heal their wounds) it may be very difficult for this person to trust in anyone, even God Himself, and at the same time the parallel is, it only takes a small thing for any trust built-up, to be knocked back down again.

We also know by experience that the psyche senses issues unconsciously and this overwhelms the already severely-traumatised areas of the brain. This fear of trust is extremely impactful on a survivor's life. Love covers a multitude of sins we are told. So we know that trust can be learned with support and an understanding of loving, trusting friends and / or lovers, slowly and carefully over time.

Distorted Emotional Regulation

We recognise that intense emotions are common with complex trauma sufferers who have survived. And ongoing abuse can cause the survivor to have many different and intense emotions. We need to normalise this for complex trauma survivors. It is so important to learn to manage and regulate the emotions which is crucial in being able to manage all of the other symptoms and accompanying problem outcomes.

There is a felt sense of Hypervigilance Around People

It is clear that the vast majority of sufferers with PTSD suffer with a hyper-vigilance, this is where the person scans the environment for potential risks and likes to have their back to the wall. However, we notice with Complex Trauma sufferers, where they often have a deep subconscious desire to understand others, having a real need to "try to work out what's going on with other people."

My own situation, growing up with a mentally ill father, who would (it seemed to me) often take pleasure in making my life miserable by taking every opportunity to smack me around the head, as I appeared to aggravate him on so many levels. I had a reason to be watchful and very aware of people's intentions, it made me feel like a bit of a gossip to other people when they noticed the way I continually watched everyone around me relentlessly, I don't feel comfortable in any restaurant and especially a bar or pub, unless I have good sight of what's coming at me. I see many non-verbal cues; I notice body language, their tone of voice, I am a great mimic, and scan their facial expressions.

Prior to my training as a psychotherapist and after completing years of personal therapy, I was able to understand myself in former years and why, many years earlier, I had classified my unusual idiosyncrasies, due to a newer often talked about pastime, that other people in my youth began to think was cool, and we talked about it, at youth clubs and when out and about.

This new idea was suddenly even trendy, though I had done it for years unwittingly. What was it? It was openly, The 'Art of People Watching', so I realise now, that I was keen to speak of this new hobby then, as I was able to hide my unconscious insecurities, within this new pastime, so easily (without fear of being seen to be neurotic, or over sensitive) It worked so well, that even I did not recognise the clues, as symptoms, of the years of continual criticism and abusive experiences.

I suffered this problem for many years and even now, though I am aware and do not talk of it readily, at times when I feel the vibe in a place is just not right, I may still feel the need to find a seat with my back to the wall and want to check out anyone near me and if I notice any threat, I have to work hard at not looking in that direction. I have found that if I am stressed, I cannot sit somewhere in public and relax, unless I have a clear view of those around me, preferably with my back covered fo safety. The uncomfortable feeling of being on view by everyone, in the middle of a crowded restaurant or bar, can exaggerate any existing stress levels, and can make me feel very insecure and disturbed, at times, that I cannot fully enjoy a meal or a quiet drink.

I also noticed, that on a day to day continuum, I may still, on an unconscious level, learn people's facial habits and their voice levels and store away, automatically what they say that could be criticism, or possible threat. I could dwell on some conversations for ages, where I may have caught someone out, on a lie, and think about it for days, and I could actually recall the exact words at length, for a long time. If anything occurred, that contradicted any of this normal data stored, it would immediately flag it up, as something potentially dangerous. I often had to stop myself checking in by saying too many times, "are you ok" to personal friends and acquaintances as a form of caretaking but it was to make myself feel more at ease to relax.

It is hard for someone to relax if they are suffering that hypervigilance internally, where they notice anyone else acting uncomfortable or upset around them. This can be exhausting at times to need to keep safe in this way. Although as a therapist, it can create a deep skillset of discernment about people. I am much better than I used to be in my earlier life and it is fairly under control these days. The aim of healing fear-based hyper-vigilance is turning it into non-fear-based discernment.

Complex trauma survivors often view the world as dangerous and people as all potentially abusive, which is understandable when having endured ongoing abuse.

There are also feelings of being remote and alone. There is a sense of feeling terribly lonely. It is painful and most survivors often feel there is very little connection and trust with people, they remain in a terrible state of loneliness, strangely, even when they are surrounded by lots of people.

It has been described as being in a bubble and it isolates you with other people. We can see each other clearly, but it seems impossible to actually connect with anyone, which often causes the sufferer to feel different as if broken, or as faulty goods, which causes a haunted feeling at times.

Promiscuity or Neediness?

Another symptom we see in the lives of those Complex Trauma sufferers, especially in those often labelled as Borderline Personality Disordered is what others may think is purely promiscuity or having many relationships always going wrong and perhaps get a sense of the sufferer's neediness. There is this need that prevails to be continually searching for a rescuer, even The Rescuer. This is obviously unconscious, where the person is looking for someone to rescue them and over time this translates into wanting to rescue others (due to their unconscious co-dependency issues). A rescuer is something many sufferers understandably think about during the ongoing trauma and this can continue on after the Trauma has ceased.

The sufferer can feel helpless and yearn for someone to come and rescue them from all the pain they feel and want them to make their lives better. This unfortunately more often than

not, leads to the sufferer seeking out the wrong types of partners or friends, especially in a toxic environment around drugs
or alcohol and night clubs, where the sufferer who is now a love
seeking addict, is often sadly being re-traumatised repeatedly
in that situation.

Trauma and the Inner child

We nearly all appear to have inner child wounds, some greater
than others. Many children who have suffered Trauma end up
with Complex Trauma and become adult survivors, but with
deep inner hurts that may continue to affect the survivor. We
know that when a child's needs are not met and when a child is
repeatedly emotionally hurt and abused, it profoundly affects
that child's developmental progress and ongoing psychological
processing long into adulthood.

A sufferer will often crave the unmet emotional needs from
their childhood, as an adult, and which can have disastrous
affects for them later as the coping solutions they act out are
not always helpful to the adult sufferer.

The Trauma sufferer with a history of coping with a neglectful
parent(s) will be still looking for security and a desire to feel
protected and held in a relationship and of being valued and
loved, as an adult. The sufferer searches for these attributes in
other adults and can be seen to be attention seeking and a trifle
needy to those who have not suffered in this way. This can also
be seen, where sufferers search for mother and father figures to
help them survive. It is also where the Love addiction drive
comes from. The desire that they will be secure and not aban-
doned that causes an obsessive like nature and may be felt to be
quite stifling and controlling for the unsuspecting new partner.

When to patient is coming for Trauma therapy we need to be
aware that Transference issues in therapy may occur and this is
normal for childhood abuse survivors and the Trauma quadrangle can sometimes be played out by sufferers as they earn to become healed survivors, this is helped by the good parent role of

the clinician therapist in these situations.

Muscle Armouring

One such symptom of this hyper-vigilance may be witnessed by sufferers as muscular tension that may excite muscles and develop them abnormally as these stressed muscles are almost always in use, they will often been seen to be gym bunnies where especially the muscle groups around the places we feel tension, such as the shoulders and neck and elsewhere in the body are developed more than usual, which almost seems like a similar trait, like some overeating, by feeding themselves excessively, in an unconscious effort to build a barrier with their own bodies, as protection from a sexual predator. Almost like a putting on a barrier, or like a suit of armour.

Obviously this may lead to many associated or referred pain issues, one woman had a neck pain that she had been seeing the neurologist for a couple of years before he sent her to me to explore psychosomatic possibilities, and it became obvious that she had Trauma and would not go for therapy and was paying the price.

This is all because the relevant muscle groups, such as facial, or neck muscles, affected in teeth grinding at night (fibromyalgia) and tension in the legs (restless leg syndrome) or pain in the abdomen and gut (IBS symptoms) or pain felt in the neck and shoulders, which often cause other symptoms of migraines and back problems. Look for the signs, as it becomes obvious to a trained clinician.

We will help patients immediately with most of these kinds of problems, using deep relaxation techniques, and predetermined gentle exercises, developed further in our Trauma work at Convergence, specifically to help in these areas of PTSD and Complex Trauma.

We also use techniques from polyvagal theory, to assess the state of the Autonomic Nervous System. We do this by simply looking at muscle actions of the Ventral Vagus nerve and checking correct actions of certain muscle groups, which we may locate at the back of the throat area and around the neck and shoulders.

We use these different forms of nerve assessments, to see the state of the autonomic nervous system, and if the tension in muscle groups are having an adverse and often painful effect on a patient, caused by nerve tensions and then the unconscious autonomic nervous tension has a knock-on effect, by feeding back to the pre-frontal and executive parts of the brain, which for some patients, we may gently massage the area to resolve migraine and offer further exercises to do at home or with another therapist, for those sufferers who have a trapped vagus nerve, usually in the neck, back, or at the cerebellum, which is causing further complications and this release of the trapped vagus nerve, usually helps a patient find tremendous relief at times.

On Dissociation

Having mentioned Dissociation elsewhere, there is also a need to explain a little more, for example, when a patient endures ongoing abuse, the brain, which is extremely powerful hardware can withdraw aspects of consciousness and facilitate dissociation as a coping mechanism and this phenomena can be over a spectrum of simple daydreaming to a more crucial form of impacting lifestyle which has been diagnosed more recently as Dissociative Identity Disorder (DID).

Obviously, in DID, this is where the brain has tried to cope with the overwhelming Trauma often in childhood abuse situations and therefore disintegration takes place, where there is a separating out that takes place, we may call this a disconnection, or split in the psyche, by an object relational part, which dissociates and forms an identity through withdrawal and develops a perspective all of its own.

We may still work with these complicated areas of Trauma and disorder by our understanding as psychotherapists and clinicians where we utilise the many tools in our psychological toolkit, such as, object relations theory and through this object relational parts therapy, we can often access the specific dissociative part(s) and work to cause a convergence of the various parts affected. It must also be said that co-morbidity is a common experience with all PTSD and Complex PTSD sufferers and should be anticipated as we look at the figure and ground of the sufferers life and symptoms of mood and the surrounding neurosis that has built up over the long term, as with Complex PTSD.

Suicidal Ideation & Self Harming

With PTSD and particularly Complex PTSD sufferers, these often have to cope with ongoing states of sadness and/or severe depression. It will therefore, come as no surprise to Trauma workers that Complex PTSD sufferers are considered a high risk by the profession, to develop suicidal thoughts.

Suicide ideation can become a way of coping, where the survivor feels like they have a way to end the severe pain, if it becomes really worse. It is important to realise that the deep emotional pain sufferers experience, can be quite unbearable and this sadly is when sufferers are at the highest risk of developing suicidal thoughts. And if that is what you or a family member is feeling right now, then please hold on, as help is only a phone, or email away. So act now, before it is too late!

CHAPTER 6:
BLOCKING &
DIFFICULTIES

I would say there are various tools we may use right now to offer relief for Trauma work, but let us look first at the blocks we may encounter in the work.

In Trauma work, I have to make decisions most days, based on what I see and know about a patient, in terms of the patient's resources and psychological strength and simple robustness or acting out that becomes more obvious as the session moves on.

I need to discern what therapy techniques may, or may not work, with this particular patient. I am often in contact with their GP by mail and will work with anyone else at the patients acceptance, such as those others in a care team; if the relevant staff behave themselves and give due respect, and I have to say, sometimes they do not, so it impossible to cooperate.

Initially, I have to assess the potential likely-hood, which there may be, regarding any attending patient unconsciously, or consciously, blocking the work we are attempting to do in Trauma therapy as there are no guarantees with what may present itself in the psyche, or the simple possibility of re-Traumatising the patient and them going away half treated or even hanging with heavy trauma symptoms; it is only the excellent training and hands-on experience which shows us the way forward in psychotherapy and particularly in the case of Trauma therapy.

Mary

When it comes to the patient being a victim of prior abuse, it is possible that the patient is doing well and healing certain Traumas, but due to the complexity of some Trauma suffering over several years we have seen evidence that the patient may revert back to a victim mode, while in therapy. This happened to me once with a middle aged woman called Mary and it was so sad to be suddenly thought of as the perpetrator because I suggested that her perpetrator should be stopped from hurting others and was she ready to call him out. Well that suddenly caused a major issue even though the perpetrator could have hurt other people, but the shame of having to speak out became so hard that the patient became neurotic again and decide to immediately stop therapy. I recall she was very angry with me for pushing the issue about stopping any further abuse.

You see a suffering patient even on the healing curve, could begin to suddenly feel let down, or even bullied (where the therapist becomes the perpetrator) from their distorted and current subjective world view of others, even feeling retaliatory toward those who are caring for them, the healers and helpers, specifically if the patient is suffering mental illness and more relevant any episodes of psychosis, or perhaps schizophrenic or paranoia states, or if they are possibly in withdrawal of chemical prescription drugs, or have other addictions and/or substance misuse.

We have to be ready to deal with the possibility of the patient 'switching' and where confusion is part of the therapy journey, one is initially and usually seen as the 'Rescuer' in the healing process and suddenly a clinician may be viewed as the 'Perpetrator', in any way, this easily disturbs the dynamic and can change into what then becomes a 'Drama Quadrangle in the psyche of the patient.

There is the perpetrator and victim then comes the rescuer and then the rescuer suddenly becomes the new perpetrator with all the baggage added from the initial perpetrator aimed at the new perpetrator, and in this dynamic the patient can get quite upset and seek sympathy form others around them, and this emotional response coupled with some manipulation, often loads the bullets for unsuspecting others to unwittingly fire. So patients can become quite malicious and we need to be ready for this.

It can also be that some patients are simply not happy with their therapy business arrangements, and may get upset, mainly due to varieties of patient eccentricities and the corresponding unreasonable expectations (something quite common and significantly prone with vulnerable adults). We recognise this reluctance to play the game or to cooperate when it comes to therapy contractual arrangements.

Some patients have unusual non-standard viewpoints or attitudes in regard to working relationships, the main problem is often around their mistrust of contracts (because they are not normally asked to sign for Government funded treatment with the GP, Dentist or Hospital though this is also changing) and just not wanting to sign their name, often due to a fear of commitment, when we are only trying to identify normal business arrangements which save future arguments or misunderstandings and helps businesses to comply with health and safety and we also need to safeguard the income of our often independent Private Practice's, or our anonymity and confidential work practices. It is also to enable business people to form a simple working alliance, but for some it's a big deal and we need to be aware of that in mental health too.

Glen

One patient Glen, who suffered with psychosis would often literally have a picture come up in his mind, of me in the form of a shark (which was upsetting for me at the time) and one has to contain feelings and humour patients at times and the outcome was a completely different life for the person concerned.

Considering this patient Glen was healed of many Traumas, life returned for the patient to a new healthy normality within a short time of three months. This client had suffered a major breakdown for two years prior to his therapy at our clinic and the outcome was a loving father and husband eventually being restored to his family and a wife left wondering why our specialised work could not be offered freely on the NHS.

I tried to break the news gently, as I explained that it is surely about money and waiting times and a reluctance to send people for Trauma work; when they have been diagnosed with psychosis or personality disorders, which in the eyes of the care teams, sadly means the NHS does not need to invest more in them, as they have come to the end of the conveyor belt treatment.

Mandy

One patient Mandy actually blocked me because it transpired she had fallen in love with me and did not want therapy to end. I was oblivious to this, at the time, of course and thought the patient was just being difficult. The mind boggles. For a woman it can also be the same in the alternative.

Kay

Then there is the lifestyle issues, where someone we shall call Kay could not continue in therapy with one of our therapists, because she explained, that she had fallen in love with her and could not continue because the therapist was hetrosexual and not gay.

There is also the need to be aware of the consequences around patients getting upset with you and the slander that may prevail through any of these types of issues, (even from a woman scorned through no fault of your own) such as having to deal with the effects of any outside criticisms of our work by family members (and particularly of unprofessional staff in mental health teams that are prone to gossip of outsiders) or other agency rumours that could be levelled at our organisation, or personal status, position. Any backlash slander needs to be met with an opportunity to talk and to examine all the facts.

Fortunately we are innocent until proven guilty in this country, but it seems to be fast changing (professionals are stood down if there are any allegations made in order to investigate allegations) with this blame culture today and unless it is life threatening or harmful to victims I believe we should be slowing down the process to jump on people and effectively close down their main form of livelihood or affect their good reputation and status, no doubt this is all part of the Nanny state we live in today.

We must safeguard ourselves against chaotic patients or of any other labels, such as those being considered as vulnerable adults, or of the patient having brain damage, or long term mental health issue, that could even be psychosis and not due to Trauma and be essentially true for a change. This type of person can also be quite damaging too.

Ben

I recall one vulnerable adult client named Ben who was a compulsive liar and I was totally unaware until a detective explained over the phone, due to a misdemeanour on Ben's part, that he had known him since he was young always in and out of trouble. He had told me he was 40 stone and presented around 14 stone at the time. Do we ever really know when someone is telling the truth? It can be difficult with sociopaths who make great con artists..

Or maybe the patient has had a psychiatric assessment and a local NHS care team are (I will not be so confident as to say 'actively') involved, by supervising their care, due to a patient that was either 'sectioned' by psychiatric staff or where the patient realised they were not coping and functioning well so had 'volunteered' themselves into care; unfortunately, in most cases, this would have happened usually because the patient was highly concerned, or under great stress and in simple confusion, and maybe felt that they could not keep themselves safe, so they admitted themselves.

Any negative criticisms of our work or indeed our behaviour might interfere with our work, as I have also experienced this in the past. Many upsets with vulnerable adults are usually just simple misunderstandings but often fuelled by other manipulative friends or family members that may have an axe to grind over some slight they felt, or misrepresentation they have picked up.

There are also obvious problems when a spouse or partner is involved in paying for our patient's therapy too, for example, if a patient suddenly is unhappy with some aspect of therapy or our attendance arrangements or have unreasonable expectations around therapy timings and progress.

When it comes to mutual confidentiality, some patients think it is alright to have more than one therapist at a time; particularly those who are extremely fearful, or suffering greatly, and no doubt these types of patients are desperate to get immediate help so they may quickly feel better, however, we cannot work this way, so when someone tells me they have a care team or when they are also seeing a psychologist or psychiatrist.

I am quite careful to remind the patient that our Trauma work is confidential and should not be discussed in any depth, I do not want my patients teaching others who are not trained how to use techniques which seem amazingly simple yet have a great deal of training in all aspects of psychotherapy. There is also my own self disclosures that need to be confidential too.

We also need to assess the possibility of undiagnosed autistic traits too (I have not been proven wrong on my assessments yet) but we do need to err on the side of caution here in making judgements without much information initially.

Our work with Trauma in the present could also be the cause of upsets. It is not unusual where patients are affected by fears or phobias. Other problems could be caused by purely uncomfortable feelings that may have been brought up in the Trauma therapy itself or even to do with any feelings the patient may need to endure while just starting to assess trauma. This is particularly noticeable if the patient is experiencing a prolonged episode of psychosis or any form of dissociation, which could be problematic in the therapy work.

In any case patients need our help. We will need to work around other care agencies, charitable, governmental, or otherwise, that might attempt to interfere with our work, unless we have met with the directors/ managers of the agencies and have a good working relationship with those who matter we need to know this is par for the course.

Your accounts or input stories could also make up the essence or content of yet another book about psychotherapy or spirituality in the future, so please keep the information and accounts coming in as it is all useful to gain needed change.

We appreciate your concerns and would value your input and therefore we are pleased to receive news from either the side of the fence, first the NHS Mental health - current care or treatment systems staff, and secondly from the Trauma sufferers, mental health patients that have been labelled wrongly and any independent counsellors, or Psychotherapist professionals.

CHAPTER 7: MORE CASE STUDIES

Here are just a few of the many case studies that show how we dealt with sufferers depending on their effects and the person concerned. Obviously names and actual events and situations have been changed just enough to protect the real patients and these patients all made a full recovery from Major Trauma.

It doesn't have to be full blown PTSD to be a Trauma worth resolving. Some Traumas have major affect and may determine a person's life, even though ALL the symptoms of PTSD are not apparent, or present at all. Post Traumatic Stress is powerful and needs to be taken seriously whatever the extent, the rule of thumb for me is. What effect is this Trauma episode having on this patient today, what energy is coming up from this Trauma, or how much is it affecting their lives from day to day, or week to week?

Esther

The first person who really surprised and encouraged me in my early Trauma work, was another (Gestalt) Psychotherapist and I am in the Integrative stream, so am also well versed in Gestalt therapy and use it a lot in my own practice and the College too!

The lady, we shall call Esther, came to me, when I was not long out of my initial Trauma training, so it is no surprise that I was feeling a little guarded and wondered why the person had come to me, when there were so many gestalt therapists out there?

The universe has this amazing way of bringing people to you

that really fit your moment and will teach you things, toughen you up and test you and will oftentimes help you, as a Master teacher will do, in your journey.

Esther was quite adamant that she wanted to work with me, she retorted that this was "because she had heard 'good things' about me" and to then add to my personal inner concerns of being good enough to sort out another therapist (yes, we all get those feelings from time to time) Esther then explained, that she had been all around the world, to USA and Europe, to get these Traumas dealt with as she was suffering PTSD and nothing had worked to remove them.

But somehow she felt I might be the one, able to help her, as I had removed Trauma from someone else she had heard of, that psychiatrists and psychologists could not appear to help from a long term mental breakdown. Well if that was not going to un-settle me, I felt at the time, nothing much else would!

The first session with Esther working with the Traumas after taking the usual time to discuss and briefly note what her main issues were and the problems we may need to resolve. She had me struggling soon after. It was beginning to be difficult just to guide this person, as she was obviously used to drama therapy in gestalt and directing her own clients, and she was finding it difficult to concentrate due to the excessive troubling Traumas and was not allowing me to work in my own way.

Having had so many experts working in this area with her previ-ously, and she knew a lot of client therapist material, about spe-cifics in giving therapy. Therefore Esther, as I suspected might happen, was beginning to attempt to take charge of the therapy direction, which was not the direction, I knew instinctively, we should go, so I needed to explain this carefully, which she ap-preciated and she recognised, so the next session we began to adjust the therapy session accordingly for me to work and we began to get results immediately. It's not always about just the 'ingredients' of the cake, it's also important how you go about cooking it.

Unfortunately, the Trauma work is not so much like normal psychotherapy, regardless of whatever your modality gravitates too. Trauma work calls for a more clinical approach, of being not only direct, but also directive and prescriptive, rather than the usual therapy way of 'being direct, but non-directive' and following the client religiously. Its like the blind leading the blind in Trauma work, though we must help the client, find their way through, together.

This work therefore requires a slightly stronger you, where you speak into the patient's life, more like a doctor would, or a hypnotherapist, with a confident authority in your voice, as you direct the patient to the external and hopefully the internal space that they need to get to.

As a Psychotraumatologist, we do need to really know what we are doing to direct the patient to where they need to be, in their thinking and emotions, at that precise time, to further enable them to get past the Trauma.

Even though, we must be quite gentle in our directives, we must not bully, but encourage the patient, in a more appropriate and determined way. Gladly, things eventually worked out with Esther, as she allowed me to direct her properly, without charging her so many thousands of pounds for therapy that didn't work.

This Trauma therapy really worked for her, so much so, that after three months Esther was completely healed of all and any shock energies previously affecting her and she then went happily on her way (beaming smiles all around) as she flitted off to her family in her home country abroad and wanted to know if I could help her, over the internet, in the future, if she needed it and perhaps also if she might refer others to me, that she specifically knew were suffering too? I was her hero and obviously agreed to help in future, if and when she might need a superhero again. All is well that ends well!

Sue

One other young women Sue, in her early thirties, explained that she had been for counselling previously to try to get resolution on something that was making her feel low and attacked her self-esteem and she had read a lot of self-help books in her quest for self-discovery, as we often may do.

But in recent years Sue openly announced to me that she had become a prostitute for a while, in her early twenties, also travelling quite a lot and being used to a risky lifestyle, but she recognised she was not really at peace and had earlier abuse issues with an older brother that she still loved which was, according to her intuition, at the root of her discomfort in life.

Sue was adamant that she had dealt with her incestuous activity with her sibling and had even forgiven him, but It eventually unravelled that he had caused her 'not to trust other men' but she was confused about that because in her mind it was dealt with (she had further concluded that she was a liberated modern woman; who knew her body well and her participating in the sex act itself was not a problem for her, (or her prostitution, obviously) even though she realised this was not good for her state of mind and she had stopped previous to attending therapy.

So Sue decided her dilemma needing to solve was something along these lines. Why was she unhappy deep down and not able to hold a relationship? Sue thought presumably, if she could switch off her feelings enough to have sex with a stranger, and without love, and feel relatively ok about it, yet at the same time could not work out what was wrong with her psychologically, where she was unconsciously cut off from feelings, which disrupted her own emotions and closed off any loving feelings shown by others which she somehow despised.

She did notice this sabotaged any possibility of close relationship and the gnawing sense of her brother was still somehow at the back of her mind, he was still in there in the mix, even though she felt she had come to terms with and accepted, the unconscious drive to sell herself; for the pleasure of others and to allow others to use her purely for sexual gratification.

Notwithstanding, the fact she knew she was also strangely drawn by this lust of intimacy, felt only in this way, but could not feel anything romantic or loving, when sex took place. She was really totally closed emotionally not knowing what love was and yet was searching but seriously could not achieve it.

What Sue did notice, was that she was angry a lot of the time with new boyfriends and would unconsciously (and at times very conscious) sabotage her potential relationships at every opportunity; especially if she really was attracted to them, but although troubled (and inquisitive as to the why) she could sincerely not link the dots, to explain why she could not allow anyone to get that close and really be able to fall in love.

Sue did know she had trust issues around men and therefore she could not trust in any man she had met, but there was this elusive underlying feeling that it had something to do with her past and perhaps even her brother?

Once we worked through the issues she said she had already had counselling for and moved on from, we uncovered the underlying Trauma associated with this situation, which was around an earlier event, whilst a child and involved her having contracted an infection which came to light due to Sue experiencing physical pain and discomfort and subsequently involved discussions with parents.

Unfortunately, Sue was covering up, for the sake of her much loved elder sibling, but then Traumatically finding out, that he was actually lying to her, when saying that he loved her and of course later this felt worse, once Sue realised as an adult, that what he was actually doing, was simply using her for sexual pleasure, so Sue's attitude to him changed somewhat and things got difficult for her to manage internally from an unconscious psychological standpoint.

The other side of the coin was his moral misguidance; in telling

Sue what to do and that he said it was ok to be sexually active and yet she knows now it was morally very wrong and it hurt her deeply; this is what surfaced eventually, being a real shock (Trauma) to her system because she loved and trusted her brother so much. Connecting with the feelings of innocence and for him to have seduced her into thinking it was ok for him to do that with her began to upset her greatly and had unconscious impacts on her levels of trust of others from then on, but they had talked it through and Sue had, in time, forgiven him for her own good, but like many others in this situation, had she really dealt with the Trauma fully?

The internalised victim and the imprinted relational philosophy of what that act had 'done to her' and what it was 'saying about her' and the way Sue then 'treated others' who longed to get close to her or those she was attracted to herself but without managing to allow them in to her heart? Sue was suffering all the more as a mature adult, now in her mid-thirties.

The good news is that the whole trust issue became something Sue could more easily deal with, once we uncovered and dealt with the initial trapped shock and after some months gained a more level playing field, so that Sue did not see every man that she was interested in and that she was attracted to and really liked, as her brother. Sue eventually reported success back to me over the internet, as she went on a long trip, this time further around the world, to also visit her parents and other parts yet undiscovered by herself. It would take further time to really heal those wounds but her resolve was strong and Sue moved on with a different philosophy eventually.

This released her emotions and understanding, at last, to become congruent and feel sincere yet controlled in her anger, as it surfaced with a target. Sue realised that she had forgiven too fast without working through the emotions around what had happened and without Trauma therapy was a tough one to deal with.

In Trauma treatment, we began to work through the situation again in therapy once the initial Trauma was effectively dealt with. Sue was now a mature adult, and could access these feelings towards her brother and see them more openly; his manipulations, the deceit and lies, there was much to discuss and uncover which was lost in time and blurred by hurt and internalised pain she had not even fully realised, which had caused those hidden but uncomfortable feelings, which she now realised were previously out of her cognitive reality for so long, this started to help her find her way back to learn to trust again.

Sue's trust issues mainly around men and her new found philosophy about men extended also through the interventions we worked on together and of the counter transference played out in the therapy room, which facilitated her change, as Sue saw me purely as just a good friendly male ally, as a man yes, but first in the role of therapist and as a more paternal figure (proffering no personal sexual attention, or demands, only giving a safe therapeutic intimacy) and only then as a wounded healer and aid. This neutral sexual perspective from a male was an unusual reaction for Sue, as she was used to a great deal of interest by red-blooded males who she reported were very attracted to her, so this immediately changed her outlook and made her feel safe. It was really refreshing to Sue, as an attractive intelligent and woman, that not everyone was only interested in seducing her, or using her as a sex object.

The whole scenario in the past had trapped the shock of reality of his lies, right there as a child, which was continually presenting (unsurprisingly) as Sue's strong lack of trust.

Sue was confused and therefore she could not previously locate this cause of her mistrust because the lines were blurred. First with her feelings of mixed confused immature emotions, as her brother gently groomed his little sister and wood her and as Sue adored her brother as her true hero giving her all the attention she needed, with an absent mother and father too busy fighting each other and trying to get ahead in the world to notice their own children's unusually close emotional relationship and her brother's systematic abuse going on at the same time.

All this was locked in Sue's mind as an adult. When she came to see me first of all, it was completely contained behind the unconscious wall of the shadow and acting out from the trapped shock that was established in her shameful acknowledgement of the event, when her mother surely discovered and at that particular moment where Sue looked to her brother and he rejected her and really lied his adolescent head off, she was only around eleven years of age and the shock of that betrayal got securely trapped in her amygdala. In reality, Sue had been systematically seduced and was ignorantly exploring and knowing herself and her brother sexually since she was around five years of age, thus distorting her respect of her own body and her emotional process of trust verses mistrust.

As Sue's therapist, it was satisfying in the end to see her blossom as a person and become more balanced as she began to contain her wild animus and feel similarly more rounded and whole as a woman; where Sue began to respect and believe in herself, as we had dealt with so much of the concealed guilt and shame this time from a cognitive and emotionally intelligent platform in the psyche. This was taking place on a different emotional level, rather than the unconscious sense of self-hatred and self-loathing.

Although morally, Sue had feelings of need that led her to promiscuity and eventual prostitution, and although making wrong choices, on another level it seemed perfectly logical to Sue in her distorted leanings towards a strengthened animus, to use her own body unemotionally, just like a man would (she thought) as her coping method, of denial, a sense of disassociation from her inner felt sense of respect for her personhood, yet there was also this inner pressure, almost need for closeness and intimacy that she temporarily gained through sexual interaction. Sue recognised that these encounters were empty but she only felt coldness in her heart and that was all there was for her at that time. Sue had previously been objectifying herself, as a mere sex toy, for those who would pay for her, which she thought was her choice, in the oldest profession in the world.

Unwittingly, Sue was a victim, by using herself this way, when she thought this was a positive personal attribute to just find and get what she wanted from men, which was unconsciously the desire to have a sense of power over men as Sue could not trust their deceitful ways and it felt good when they desired her and therefore she saw herself elevated in their eyes, as an object of desire and worthy from a physical perspective and all the time still looking for love and true intimacy, but never finding it through physical attractions and sex.

When we finished therapy, Sue explained she was able to eventually have a more intimate emotional experience and started to settle with a new partner, which initially felt strange to her with this man, but Sue knew she was on a healing journey now and looked forward to a safer walk with all other prospective male friends in the foreseeable future and therefore considered the prospect of understanding and maybe experience what love really consists of and perhaps finding the mature love I spoke to her of in session, rather than sadly having only sexual exploits with no deep feelings attached.

Sue was also encouraged as she learned the potential in her shadow when she began to recognise and find out about her unique soul qualities and ideals, she began to reconnect with her heart (her spirit) she was hoping perhaps to find her true self and then seek her true soul mate and finally settle down. Sue went away, hopeful of a brighter future, without the toxic shame weighing her down, she felt somewhat liberated at last.

Lorna

Another person with complex Trauma called Lorna, had a great deal of problems with flashbacks. She had suffered a violent childhood with a Father who was incredibly prone to fits of rage and lashing out towards her and her siblings. There was also a problem with neglect and an over sexualised childhood in the past, with several rapes involved from an early age.

Lorna was abused over and over again and to make matters worse, those in positions of authority such as the police, the courts, social workers, counsellors, psychologists, and including her parents, unwittingly sometimes, all let her down at important and traumatising events I her life, she realises now that this resulted in Complex PTSD and she received the usual label administered to her, Borderline Personality Disorder, due to her unusually bad behaviour, while she was trying to make sense of the world that was so hostile towards her and accusing her of wrong and deeply hurting her, without really recognising her agonising childhood or noticing the hell she was currently going through, or even simply taking into account her traumatic past and Traumas she suffered over a long time period.

Lorna had been through the NHS mental health and social workers care, on her journey from adolescence to parenthood and beyond, within the overall context of care by the authorities and the NHS, usual 'Conveyor Belt therapy' (CBT).

There were many times when Lorna just collapsed in grief and hopelessness, where she would be flooded with tears of anger and disbelief, in the way her life had to be lived previously and resentful at the treatment she had endured, by those who should have cared for her.

In therapy and out of it Lorna struggled with her emotions to contain and experienced many fits of temper and screaming fits outside of therapy, towards those she felt had dismissed, or ignored her, or worse, those who had continually broken her boundaries.

We know there are several types of flashbacks and Lorna had all three types present in her neurosis. Lorna experienced Emotional Flashbacks which are usually prevalent with all PTSD survivors. She had to deal with all three, and we will show all three of types.

There are Visual Flashbacks. This is where Lorna suddenly would have an image flash up of something that she experienced and instantly recalled. This often happens to women in their 4o's who may have suffered child abuse at some point in time and they had largely pushed it to the back of their minds and suddenly it appears, whilst getting on with their daily lives. It can be terrifying as it seems to violently appear out of nowhere. Where Lorna's mind was triggered and she was transported back to the Trauma, she felt like she was reliving it fully, at that point.

The she would get Somatic Flashbacks. Again this is described when Lorna felt body sensations, often with deep pain and discomfort, in different areas, all of which were affected by the Trauma. These pains and sensations can't be attributed to any other problems in the health of the patient, but rather they are triggered by something that creates the body to "feel" the trauma again. The body remembers!

Then Lorna would, at times, feel the powerful Emotional Flashbacks. These are the flashbacks that are less known and understood, but these flashbacks appear to be the most prevalent of them all in complex Trauma. Lorna experienced these Traumas, where the emotions from the past were often triggered. Many sufferers do not really understand these intense emotions are actually flashbacks in memory we believe the Amygdala throws up, coupled with this, we often notice that there is a great deal of emotional irrationality shown in the Patient when this is going on.

Trauma therapy continued for about six months or more and there were major breakthroughs and healing took place. Then we began the long road to recovery and the suffering began to be surviving and reappraisal of so many things in her life. She is currently working through many issues that still surface from time to time and will be helpful to her clients as a wounded healer as she continues her healing journey and desire to help others, no doubt originally produced from the co-dependency issues nearly all carers have that drives them to help others and rescue anyone who seeks their help.

Martin

There was also a man we shall call Martin who suffered ADHD and came for Trauma work feeling highly anxious even to travel to the therapy. He was able to explain that he had been hit around the head in an assault outside his work place one day and that had caused him to be terrified of going out in the street at any time and he had flashbacks and nightmares and could not relax for any length of time, his heart would madly race and he would become so anxious, that he thought he was going to have a heart attack.

Martin could not concentrate at work and realised he had become quite irritable and snappy and this was affecting his relationship with his colleagues at work and his girlfriend when he saw her as well.

Martin and I discussed the criminal case around his assault and the crown prosecution service had enough evidence already (to prosecute the perpetrators in his case) so we did not need to worry about his memory of the event fading, or blurring in any way that might prejudice the case proceedings and that we did not remove any main detail from his mind before the statements and proceedings had been completed for the police investigations and the courts.

With my © Virtual Brain Re-Set therapy it is known that when we remove Trauma energy that details come very clear but after the therapy they fade just as quickly, but in this case it did not matter and would not effect the case in court so we proceeded with the Trauma work.

After approximately six Trauma sessions with me, he was able to find a sense of norm once more and we removed these major Trauma issues and talked of other worrying feelings he had around his injuries and the prognosis of long recovery and Martin was able to return to work as almost a new man psychologically, if not physically, at last. Things had settled down and he could concentrate once more and do his job and have a healthy relationship once more.

Tina

Another person we shall call Tina, had gambling problems and run up huge credit card debts her husband had to pay for, it transpired the Traumatised woman had suffered childhood sexual abuse by her uncle and her way of unconsciously dealing with it, was to gamble and needed to feel she won when the problem all along was the Complex Trauma issues and when we dealt with the Trauma she was clear of the gambling once more. Unfortunately, there were complications later in therapy where I was placed in a drama quadrangle and she began to have other anxieties, mainly relating to her father and the family, but these were self-inflicted because of her co-dependency issues and she went into a decline and left therapy before we finished helping her. You cannot win them all!

Diana

There was another young woman who came to me, that could not really talk or express herself in the initial therapy sessions and I had to ask questions all the time to attempt to open her up to normal discussions, we shall call her Diana and she was in a relationship that did not appear to be going anyweher fast and I noticed that although she was very closed and appeared to have difficulty getting into her feelings, nevertheless she showed that she was quite intelligent. You would not have known that, apart from her writing level, as she would answer "I don't know" to practically anything you asked her, regarding her childhood, her life generally, her feelings around work, her feelings towards her family, or what she wanted from therapy, or what had happened to her or what her feelings were about almost anything.

She appeared to have no opinion about anything. After Trauma sessions she blossomed suddenly like someone opened the flood gates and she talks without hesitation and contributes a great deal to a conversation at any level. She lost the don't knows and has opinions and has taken charge of her life at last.

One year later she was a dynamo and although still a little cut off from her feelings and still acting out a little, Diana was really showing her intelligence but not her potential as she still doubted herself in many ways, but she is continuing in therapy and there is more light at the end of the therapy.

Can Traumas be dealt with quickly now?

How many sessions do patients need and how quickly are patients able to get past their Trauma and on with their daily lives? I may answer this question easier with examples, by offering a couple of case studies with patients attending my Trauma practice, experienced over the past few years. Obviously names and details have been changed in important areas to safeguard these individual's identities.

Lauren

Lauren was an intelligent University student who had been recently raped. This was presented initially as a single Trauma that was keeping her from her studies at university and she could not concentrate for more than a few moments before the whole traumatic event was crashing into her conscious mind once more. Therefore as you would imagine Lauren was finding it hard to sleep at night as this had happened in her own bed and found she had become hyper-vigilant around any man she met since that awful time.

I explained to Lauren on the phone that we would probably deal with the 'shock' of the rape with only one or two sessions of therapy and I would not need to know any details, but then if she wanted to continue in therapy, once the shock was dealt with, we would then no doubt be able to talk about the issues around the shame effects and any fear held, or the self-esteem issues and some of the lasting effects of what the rape psychologically said about her. It was explained all this could be worked through when she became more confident with the shock lifted but Lauren was told she did not need to continue after the Trauma therapy if she didn't feel comfortable to continue. She agreed to an appointment and duly came into see me almost immediately to deal with the Trauma effects.

As I promised Lauren, we dealt with the rape quite fast; in her case it was only one double session. A major single Trauma event like this, we deal with quickly and it is quite a normal experience in Trauma therapy today.

Remember, we need to take time for the patient to be shown and guided through some relaxation exercises, as preparation prior to the therapy work and then once the Trauma work is finalised, then we need to take more time afterwards, because many are quite relieved and ready to discuss their feelings once they feel such immediate relief. Lauren was able to get some sleep at last and managed to easily resume her studies the following week.

The question posed in this scenario is; Did Lauren need more Trauma therapy, well she thought it was helpful to look at other events in the past, but maybe in the great scheme of things some would say this extra work was unnecessary, but we are client led to a certain degree and I agreed it was going to be helpful to clean out the closet if she was willing to go there.

Lauren agreed that it was a good idea to talk to me more and perhaps deal with other underlying issues around this situation and her sexuality. We were able to meet regularly afterwards and she managed to get her university to pay for a few sessions on their student liability insurance policy and associated care plan which worked well in her favour to deal with any unconscious remaining feelings and thoughts that might encroach on her in the future.

It further transpired that Lauren had other events in her life that surfaced around sexuality and problems with men that we eventually dealt with in that time and she was able to resume a normal life once more, so we had a happy ending to this crippling Trauma event for this young woman and it was all over within a few months and we parted amicably, job done.

In this event, Lauren was able to work through other feelings of lack of self-worth, which was brought up by this event, as her unconscious shadow surfaced and unsettled her, but no doubt she could have gone away after the initial main Trauma shock was dealt with and still coped satisfactorily with life from then on. Without it she would no doubt have suffered long and hard.

The point I make here is that many one off major Traumas, like accidents, or violence or deaths or anything that shocks us in any main way, and we do not know who will succumb until it happens.

Some are more susceptible than others and those we think are weak endure and those who purport to be strong are suddenly and mysteriously engulfed with the 'fight or flight' mechanism within the autonomic nervous system's hot-wired defence programme (through a big shock, or several shocks) to develop full blown PTSD.

Some suffer what we may call Complex PTSD, this is something that usually develops from a series of shocks over a protracted time period, which could be many years. It can certainly happen with systematic abuse for many years, which could be physical abuse, in some direct way, or psychological abuse perhaps within a family situation as children of a violent parent or in a violent marriage.

There are many ways we may suffer complex problems over long periods. We never know the extent or the effect of prolonged Trauma, but it is the aftermath of the resolution the TPP, that can mean longer times in therapy enabling effective healing to take place, where the past is affecting the present.

This may well also happen with someone who presents as a very strong person psychologically. Maybe a bit of a hard man (like a hardened marine sergeant) or a seasoned journalist covering war zones, or a fighter pilot flying many missions and seeing comrades die, or a violent criminal who is always hanging around gangs and witnesses many atrocities, or a prize fighter hanging up his gloves. It may happen at any time to anyone. We never know when PTSD will strike.

CHAPTER 9: STAGES OF TRAUMA

Where someone experiences Trauma, the traumatic events vary so much with individuals.

To prove a point, let me explain something that happened to my self and two other friends of mine.

I recall one actual situation, where I was out volunteering with a homeless patrol with the Street Ministers one Saturday evening, along with two other friends and we were patrolling the night club district, on the streets around where we live, in an effort to put something back into society and simply caring for the disenfranchised and our younger generation and to be available to them in a pastoral way, giving support to vulnerable individuals; literally by just being there and available in the night time economy often just befriending and calming people down, or at times just looking after people, worse for wear, and to aid the Police patrols at times allowing them to get on with tackling crime.

We were also attempting to be a listening ear and help for the homeless, or where occasionally the younger clubbers found themselves in trouble, or perhaps really needed to talk to someone who was non-judgemental and caring.

At times we were able to take the load off of the Police and used as an aid to their work, by being on site caretakers for them while they waited, either for an ambulance, or expecting a parent driving in to pick up and take them home. Then we were suddenly traumatised ourselves.

We saw an event from three different geographical points which altered our perspective of the particular event, as we were stretched out about 15 metres apart, where all arrived to a situation, where one male clubber had gotten out of hand with his girlfriend and was suddenly grabbed and held by four burley security guards, and with his hands vertically outstretched, they appeared to have been frog marching him away from the doors of the venue into the alley and suddenly there was more struggling and commotion, then we noticed a person hit the clubber on the back of the head with his heavy two way radio and noticed the clubber go down on the floor and was left to recover.

A short while later as we were concerned for the man's welfare, he had not moved far and it was obvious that he was in trouble, so we motioned to the Police and they also moved in and then began to help the man to on his feet, but he immediately collapsed and began to jerk around, he was obviously fitting.

An ambulance was called and we kept in contact with the Police as we were concerned that things needed to be reported from reliable witnesses with clear heads, such as ourselves, as we had not been drinking on duty.

What transpired, according to our first volunteer, moving closest to the event and farthest from the two of us following, was that the clubber had been struggling like crazy and was hurling abuse at the security staff and in their opinion was obviously threatening to do something violent to them if he got free and the man who hit him was trying to subdue him and help his security friends not come to harm.

The two of us standing further away didn't see it that way at all and it traumatised us a great deal, when we realised what transpired from that strike to the man's head (we were rightly concerned) whilst another standing closer also saw the action up close and the struggle that we never realised, yet for us two friends, it was really traumatic as it appeared to be totally unwarranted and the man was clearly hurt badly.

Unfortunately the man went to hospital and suffered brain damage and was comatose for three months and has not yet fully recovered from that event.

The first volunteer was not traumatised, but our other volunteer with me was very traumatised and could not go out again and got sick even thinking about it and I myself was traumatised, but had immediate trauma therapy and recovered fast and was able to attend and volunteer more without further problems.

CHAPTER 10: VARIOUS TREATMENTS

Treatments available today

We wish to suggest some of the treatments that are offered not for you to go for those treatments but to compare notes and then to choose the best possible treatment for you.

When you are struggling with major Trauma and diagnosed either rightly, or wrongly today, by others, you may be told by your GP, etc, or counsellor that you may have 'Post Traumatic Stress Disorder' (PTSD) in which case the referral through your doctor to the NHS would then point you in the way of the NICE guidelines anti-dote of treatment which is mainly 6 weeks of their Cognitive Behaviour Therapy (commonly called CBT) which we also use for normal therapies.

But as far as major Trauma is concerned, it is more what I would challenge to be renamed as a 'Conveyor Belt Therapy' (which is as good as a chocolate teapot for Major PTSD Trauma) or if you are incredibly fortunate, and find someone who is not just ticking boxes for a living, where they may be taking you seriously for a change and send you for treatment with someone in the NHS, trained in the use of 'Eye Movement Desensitisation and Reprocessing (commonly called EMDR).

Welcome to the 'long wait therapies' in the NHS, usually 9 months here for CBT and 18 months for EMDR or ASD assessments, but please remember the good news here, which is, that we trained, qualified and either registered and/or accredited independent psychotherapists are out there somewhere, ready and able to offer help too, which they wont refer you too, and it is usually much faster to access and usually more effective, regardless of the NHS propaganda mantra, that 'CBT, is evidence based' and obviously they have been brainwashed into thinking it is the only effective therapy of the day, yeah right! Is that like the evidence based 'diagnosis labels', in the Psychiatric Manuals, then? Most of these spurious labels are now being hotly challenged in psychotherapy circles right now, as we write. You couldn't make it up, could you? However, there are always exceptions to the rule and with a wry wink, we may say, no guarantees offered from anyone, obviously.

But if you are struggling with Complex Post Traumatic Stress Disorder (C-PTSD), there is still hope and help is available to you here (not commonly found in the NHS, unless you want another 6 weeks CBT, winks again, Oops!, (I am having to sarcastically wink so much about the NHS, that I am beginning to think perhaps I have a tick in my eye).

These are the authorised common treatments for PTSD. GP's tend to immediately prescribe 'Drugs' to help you with the anxiety, but seriously try to get help before taking them unless you are feeling suicidal. Then there is the raw EMDR therapy, which may be accompanied by drugs alongside it, and there is the old favourite, CBT. There is also a form of desensitising therapy through meditation to recall good memories to distract, or using music to relax and smelling perfume. Then there is also something called Schema Therapy, which can be helpful for people with C-PTSD. Parts therapy is used and our own recommended CBPT and CET therapy, developed here in UK.

Drugs?

It may be too little and too late, but it is high time we stood up for wisdom and common sense ethics and morals within this country and stop playing into the hands of the elite nanny state morons who couldn't 'organise a 'proverbial' - drinking party, within a brewery!'.

Much of what goes on in the world of political correctness extremes and so the called 'minority' and media style outbursts makes no sense to the common rank and file man in the street.

Such a ludicrous situation we are in today where we trust in the NHS driven by the greed of these major drug cartels that we believe influence the BMA greatly and determine the Journal's mandates for doctors to adhere to, with all the big money behind it all, and then the GP's simply become drug pushers in the name of medical care proffering these drugs to poor unsuspecting patients who find themselves becoming hooked on pain killers, anti-depressants and sleeping pills instead of finding ways to access professional mental health therapists.

Thankfully things are beginning to change and some patients who are attending Trauma therapy have begun to think twice before taking these anti-depressants.

Some GP's are now also looking to alternatives but are not too popular with those powers that be. I am sure I won't be too popular either when this message goes out to those who are heading the corrupt and nonsensical system that really stinks whilst it poops on the suffering, as a quick fix; when they could be really helped long term instead.

CAT & Schema Therapy – in depth CBT and Re-Parenting

This is something we do here, after the main Traumas are dealt with sufficiently to remove the trapped shock(s). This is for those who need some "reparenting," or to learn new life-skills, which takes us back to typical psychotherapy parent / child transference and counter transference issues.

This is useful to impart new wisdom and to be present as the good parent. We have both men and women ready to offer these re-parenting skills to nurture patients and help them to re-wire their limiting introjects from biological parents who unfortunately, caused damage, so obviously got it wrong at some point.

It may be helpful as we can engage in this type of schema therapy which is called "limited reparenting therapy. By all accounts, we believe the International Society of Schema Therapy, suggest that limited reparenting, is when a therapist takes on a trustworthy parent-like role (within the bounds of a professional relationship) in treatment, so the client can learn what a safe and trusting relationship looks like, something we do as part of our integrative psychotherapy in Convergence.

Please "Don't suffer in Silence! So, please, please, Do let your fear come into the light of day, by finding real Trauma therapy that works.

Talking to other people about what it is that you struggle with may help, or in our experience, it usually may just re-traumatise you to do that, especially if you have full blown PTSD or C-PTSD. Just like the old idea of debriefing Air Force Pilots, or maybe Police officers and other front-liners suffering Traumatic times and events, it just did not work and caused them to eventually close up and repress the information and continue to suffer internally until they died. What a shame!

But you cannot heal behind closed doors, self-help books may only help to around 20% of any suffering or to gain emotional intelligence, so take a risk and realise you need real help to gain lasting relief and NO MORE TRAUMA needs to be felt!

We also teach ways to Self-Soothe

We recommend ways to psychotherapy patients with all sorts of anxiety related conditions including depression which is also usually brought on by anxiety through worry and they learn to incorporate self-soothing techniques into their lives, so if you live with C-PTSD. We will show some techniques that may help patients to cope. This is the first:-

The Benson technique

We teach patients to use the Benson technique, this is simply healthy breathing in and out first of all to get the airways open and to allow oxygen to flow properly.

It is scientifically proven and in laymen's terms, it will help to engage the parasympathetic nervous system, which works to calm you down and it will release the right chemicals into your brain, to calm you down.

So try to get into a sense of 7/11 breathing. The most important aspect is to get into a comfortable rhythm of breathing.

You breath in to the count of seven and you breath out to the count of eleven. Try to breath out through the nose as a longer outbreath. The idea being, if you have nose blockage problems, or even simply a cold, you may usually be able to breath out through the nose, even if you can't breath in through your nose at times. This can work well with patients that may be having a panic attack where it has been possible to help them, at times, even over the phone. This works really well.

If you have chest breathing problems and find it difficult, then just try a breathing rhythm of 5/9, or even 3/7 to start with; where you use the full chest and abdomen to breath. Some people call this belly breathing, but it is a little more complete than that. We suggest you become aware of your breathing and practice this at all times.

We utilise a Convergence 'Safe Place' Induction

We recommend a particular meditation technique which takes a patient deeper into meditations and brings much more of a calming effect than usual meditation on things around you. We call this the Convergence 'Safe Place' Induction.

We can offer a guided Convergence Induction to create something completely new for a patient, who may struggle with the idea and perhaps they are not used to suing their imagination positively, as historically they perhaps cannot find a safe, or even a truly calming place, without negative involvements attached to it, from their past.

This is something the patient is then taught to do for themselves especially before bed at night and at all other times when they are feeling stressed in some way. Obviously, the more they practice, the better it works for them. People who sometimes say I tried that it didn't work usually never persisted past the first or second time and therefore never found the rewards of using their imagination positively and usually let their intrusive thoughts and negative imagination take over without a fight back, as normally happens with OCD sufferers, who may also be experiencing Trauma.

We are always more likely to follow the directions of someone offering treatment when they are in front of us leading and teaching, as it feels more personable and therapeutic to be closer to a therapist and hear their soothing words.

Develop Positive self-talk

Rehearsing 'positive self-talk' is so important and to stop the negative self-talk. What we need to understand is this is literally a form of cognitive hypnotherapy in action as we go about our daily lives. We either use our imagination positively to help us or we literally talk ourselves into a hole, so to speak.

This positive self-talk especially in the mirror, to yourself, can be an amazing way to progress against negative thoughts about yourself and the world around you.

For example, a common automatic thought from someone who suffers from C-PTSD is, 'I shouldn't trust others,' "When you practice positive self-talk like, 'I am safe,' or 'I will be OK' and 'I can do this,' it's possible to have a profound positive impact on your thinking and the way you engage with the world around you.

Allow yourself to Feel

Learning to feel and identify your feelings can be quite challenging, but it is so important if you have repressed your feelings, to allow yourself to feel. And to tell yourself you will not die. This is the death instinct and we need to overcome this situation. We may be feeling overwhelmed emotionally and need to reassure ourselves, that it is ok, to feel the feelings and that we are going to be able to cope with this overwhelming sadness, anger, shame, or possibly guilt, or even heartache, or whatever it is, sad, mad, glad, or bad.

If you struggle to feel your feelings, you're not alone. This is what we help with every day as psychotherapists. If this is you, seek support from a mental health professional, if you need help with this. You can also check out the following stories from our Mighty community that may be relatable:

We help patients to journal their Healing journey

We use lots of different ways to enhance a patient's journey and one way is to reflect on the journey itself which can be quite enlightening and encouraging to patient and therapist alike. We obviously use feedback forms for the basics, but we also recommend mood journaling (not a diary) and on top of that, as a direct response to therapy interventions and 'aha!' moments.

We ask patients to reflect midweek and write out what they felt that they received in therapy within session each time and whatever they worked through afterwards on their own.

Journaling, is particularly helpful as It covers your entire therapy journey and is useful to look back on that amazing healing journey and reflect on how you coped at certain times. Such as what you learned from the times you gained help and learned to cope in difficult situations you faced. Obviously we keep an account of what happened along the way from our perspective, but your reflections and understandings are the most important for you to learn.

Are we there yet? To record your mental health journey is a great way to celebrate recovery milestones. If you struggle with follow-through on tracking, ask your therapist to provide support and a sense of accountability.

At the same time it is very common for people suffering C-PTSD to think the worst of themselves and discredit their positive steps and growth achieved, it's helpful to go back and read your own words and look at your personal progress.

The body remembers

We also know when animals are traumatised, such as when they are darted to put them under anaesthetic when they awake the first thing they tend to do is to stand up and then invariably, with the main danger passing, they just vigorously shake their bodies, before running off.

Research shows trauma affects the body physically and for this reason we also recommend engaging with your body physically and you can literally stand and shake off that trauma (trapped shock) energy and to then also self-soothe in those tougher moments, to breath and talk to yourself in a nurturing way and to even physically begin to embrace and stroke yourself calmly.

Identify which feelings are coming up and address them via exercise. For example, if you are experiencing anger, go for an intense run. If you're feeling restless anxiety, consider renting a kayak for the afternoon. Eventually, you'll begin to feel the benefits of mindful exercise and even crave it as a way to keep your mind and spirit right.

Try to educate yourself psychologically

An important key to recovery and emotional intelligence so we know where to start is learning more about C-PTSD and how it manifests.

My other smaller book on Anxiety, Fears and Phobias on Amazon is also a useful companion read for those suffering Trauma PTSD and C-PTSD too, etc. We also run several One Day Seminars and Workshops, to cover many psychological problems which are found on our web site and advertised through our email newsletter sent out regularly to subscribers. See web site at www.convergencecollege.org. for more details and to subscribe. We are also on facebook. Just search for - 'Convergence College'.

We also recommend reading Pete Walker's book, "Complex

PTSD: From Surviving to Thriving" and the writings and teachings of Bessel Van Der Kolk are very good too.

CHAPTER 11: CONVERGENCE THERAPY

The © *Virtual Brain Re-Set* ™

Don't get me wrong here. We are not talking about a benign memory now, but the malignancy of the trapped shock effect. The **bad shock,** as it used to be called, in days gone by, the Traumatic event(s) causes the memory to get stuck in a 'fight or flight' affect and once the **shock is removed** (not simply minimised) the memory is released from the cycle of crisis, where it is **trapped** or **stuck** and then becomes just another memory. The memory is filed in the executive part of the brain the way you would do in an office filing system. We place it in another completed file. Perhaps metaphorically refiling it after it has been completed where it goes into the section marked *'miscellaneous memories that were hurtful at the time'* under file number...

You see we get rid of the **shock** and the remaining memory is harmless. It may not be pleasant still, but it becomes harmless and is a 'complete new story' that has now been dealt with,

from that treatment time onwards and made healthy again.

The best way to describe the way we work with Trauma is by explaining a little more of our Convergence College Training approach to Psychotherapy. The © **Virtual Brain Re-Set** ™ which utilises our Convergence psychotherapy systems approach and is best explained with the brand word **Convergence** as we employ a five-fold integrative holistic model which best describes the charism that drives us.

We call this our new 'integrative' system as the new kid on the block and it delivers so much today and is so completely integrative that we use the word 'Convergence' to sum it up.

This new *Convergence Psychotherapy* is an integration of many other theoretical models used in psychologies and the new '*NeuroSomaSocioPsychoSpiritual*' System has been developed and used as a complete and powerful approach, to client and patient work, in all our current psychotherapy training methods at Convergence College.

With certain forms of PTSD, such as sufferers of extreme child abuse, with many Traumas and protracted periods of Traumatic interactions experienced, or with prolonged combat Trauma, we believe that there is a need to work with gentler 'less re-traumatising methods', such as Convergence By-Pass Therapy (CBPT) where we take the Trauma re-engagement, in session, down to around only 25% negative energy focus while in the Trauma therapies.

We prefer this gentler two tier approach in the © **Virtual Brain Re-Set** ™ Therapy of our Convergence methods utilising our CBPT first as a gentler method of relaxation and imagination in meditations and inductions which allows easy access to specific traumatic events on a lower intensity level to begin with and then utilising the CET HIT Therapy to deal with what we term the sludge of the Trauma affect causing unconscious levels of changed behaviour and philosophies in relationship, particularly around trust levels and self-image and self-confidence as well as the often unconscious accompanying, acting out, where we tackle the Trauma affect in a more direct way.

This later method is also offered to patients to find and uncover hidden Traumas when all the cognitive ones have been efficiently removed in our process, rather than going in to Trauma inhumanely like a bulldozer, where we perhaps find unmasked detail and horror felt within the trapped shock energy, experienced in the amygdala fight or flight;

And the raw image details that are usually experienced with immediate and impacting EMDR which can reach levels of up to 85% re-traumatisation of patients, while in session undergoing the Trauma therapy.

At Convergence we access these individual Traumas; first by gaining patients trust and using calming techniques to gain stability.

One of our therapies is CBPT which facilitates deeper relaxation and utilises a controlled Convergence Induction, including trained biofeedback therapy (which reduces the nervous state substantially and aids the Trauma reduction) and then by using deep meditative states we may rework the original narrative of the trauma, or using CET whilst eye spotting, through the optic nerves, we find sections of traumatised areas in the brain where the 'trapped shock' is situated and the main Trauma energy may be released through our virtual brain reset technique.

This enables the amygdala to return to a normal autonomic nervous system reaction which is also backed up using bilateral sound and polyvagal exercises to further calm the brain for reset and bring the ventral vagus nerve, back into a natural state of calm. This system safely removes all Traumas over a short time frame and the beauty is we do not need to know details of the Trauma initially until after a person has been de-traumatised and then we may deal with guilt and shame that may surround Trauma abuse, or the horrors of any violence incurred, etc.

Of course we employ extra methods in our therapies which enable further calming psychologically by the therapist's own hippocampus as there is a sense of peace and safety projected out. The other calming could also be gained by further help (as previously explained) from animal involvement such as with the equine / canine time out.

We therefore work hard with our CBPT to lessen the impact of discomfort with our Patients to start with in Trauma therapy and due to the gentler approach we do not need to know the gory details of the Trauma being treated in therapy sessions.

We will then treat any patient's shame or guilt, associated with their Trauma suffering, in later regular sessions when we are treating the change of relational philosophy that accompanies nearly all major Trauma sufferers, once the Trauma shock has been removed and the Trauma/s have been resolved sufficiently and then we have a level playing field to work without fear of re-traumatising a patient.

We must mention that, even though the 'shock' is swiftly removed from the traumatic incident(s) when we employ the 'Virtual Brain Reset' with Trauma sufferers, there is almost instant relief, where the patients are cooperating, by not blocking the bad or difficult memories.

This cooperation is not difficult for the patient to engage with, because we explain fully what a patient needs to do, to help the process, rather than to oppose and restrict the process of healing and inadvertently block what we are doing by not following the very simple instructions given, or not trusting that we are able to remove the trauma shock, in the resetting treatment, which will move them forward through and past any traumas, Obviously we work at the patients pace. These are some of the methods we employ to help sufferers.

One way, that most prefer, is the regular and natural way we work, in the two tier system of shock removal. This is where we obviously act cautiously and sensitively in our normal routines and the way we offer the treatments.

Trauma treatment is initiated by the assessment appointment and after we demonstrate to the patient, the best way to ground and nurture, using a safe place, they usually learn fast how to reduce anxiety in readiness. We do not believe we should just give the client an App to go away and do it without teaching and encouragement and to explain why we are doing it. We then help the patient work with their anxiety levels, through the following week, to be more comfortable to work with us.

Therefore we have instigated one week of relaxation techniques that is taught and suggested to complete each night before sleep and anytime through the day, if anxiety levels begin to increase.

We have several psychological treatment methods, using various techniques, to deal with the trauma-shock in the events. Some therapists only have one way to deal with traumas and are stuck when it does not work so they have to refer on. We have many tools in our psychological bag of trauma treatments, unlike other lesser experienced therapists.

For the brave and the impatient, we have other ways to work, where we would expect the patient to bite the bullet and get it over with fast and where the trauma shock is brought out like a tooth being extracted and then It's all over, bar the shouting. This method is a bit raw and that means we expect it to be more intense for a shorter period. The most important aspect is that we will go with the patient's directives and meet them with compassion and professionalism at every level.

Dependent on the assessment of the patient's level of Trauma and the anxiety the patient is experiencing, will determine what we will suggest, as the best way forward for each patient. One size does not fit everyone. We will arrange a treatment plan to tackle the trauma(s) for each individual person.

What usually happens within the very first treatment, using our tried and tested interventions in the Trauma therapy, is almost immediate relief after a short intense period of ten to fifteen minutes. Some trauma shocks may take a little longer to reduce in intensity, but the trapped shock will almost certainly reduce in the very first intervention unless the patient is blocking. 95%

of people cope with the short time of discomfort and we are able to deal with it immediately and safely, the patient will then feel immediate relief.

Some patients even cry after the treatment (with relief) and suddenly can feel very tired, because they have been so keyed up, for so long, that the body is like a wound spring and once we have taken the shock away and it goes forever, then they can relax and the tiredness comes on them and they will often yawn and stretch. It is good to be brought to therapy by a friend or partner when suffering with trapped shock, so the patient does not have to drive home very tired or even feeling exhausted afterwards. This is a serious business.

Everyone is different, and patients sometimes get frightened and start to block, so we concentrate on teaching the patient to relax and use techniques at home for a week before coming for the treatment and that alleviates much of the anxiety around the Trauma so that we may work sensitively and safely with sufferers.

However, the shock is dealt with but there are memories around the event, that may become a little raw, so the processing time sometimes continues over the next few days, immediately after trauma treatment, but the shock is gone and the memories reduce in intensity so that the patient feels ok to think about them at last.

The shock has gone, but the treatment often brings up details within the treatment as it is being worked on, some details may have previously been hidden from conscious memory. There are many stories of what suddenly comes into view when in the treatment process, as the initial processing brings details, from the traumatic memories and makes them reasonably vivid, for a short while, some details may become more obvious, details that were not conscious before.

That can mean patients suddenly realise and identify the event situation, like the colour of the curtains, or carpet or some other fact emerges and it was not quite as they thought it was. Perhaps not so terrifying after all but the Amygdala had such a grip on the patient that they could not be aware, that it was not so bad after all. The patient's mind was gripped with fear and the logic had gone out of the window and the person was trapped in their own emotions, all the while, it had not been fully dealt with.

When it comes to bad memories, usually, these memories begin to fade very soon after and philosophy changes. It is often reported back, once the trapped shock has been removed, that the eventful original memories of many traumas just disappear, because the shocking events have been resolved, and then the memories are no longer found and they are completely gone from the mind. It is simply amazing how the mind can let go once the shock is removed.

CHAPTER 12: PTSD & FLASHBACKS

We are still only touching the surface of the science in the complexities of the brain and therefore Complex PTSD is, until now, a relatively new arena of psychology.

However, we do know this at least, the root of complex post-traumatic stress disorder (C-PTSD) develops from enduring complex trauma. So complex trauma is ongoing, or repeated interpersonal trauma.

In one sense we perceive this from the perspective, where the victim in this shocking situation is traumatised in a trapped situation, where the victim is for all intents captive, where there appears no recognisable way to escape.

When we think of child abuse that is ongoing, there is entrapment, which has now been given the description 'captivity abuse' because the abused child simply cannot escape.

And we may see the same situation in domestic violence, which is another typical example. There is a great deal of people involved in forced prostitution and sex trafficking which is another form of shocking enslavement.

What do we know about Complex PTSD? It has not been officially accepted as a separate disorder yet. But as far as those who recognise it as such Complex PTSD is a proposed disorder which is different to post-traumatic stress disorder.

We do know that many of the issues and symptoms experienced by the suffering survivors of complex trauma have a different set of symptoms.

The list, of symptoms, within the (uncomplicated) PTSD diagnostic criterion, are usually there, but to a lessor or greater extent, and yet there is so much more going on internally.

We recognise that trying to understand something we call Complex PTSD helps to differentiate the differing other experiences and can validate these added symptoms so that sufferers are not wrongly assessed.

The impacts of a sufferer experiencing Complex Trauma is very different to a one time or short lived trauma. The effect of repeated and ongoing trauma which has been caused by perpetrators makes changes in the brain, and also changes the sufferer at a basic core level. This changes their philosophy of the way sufferers view the world, including other people and themselves in very profound ways.

We also acknowledge that there are also many self-help strategies, some we teach, to manage the symptoms and help heal. We also need to train therapists to treat sufferers with a great deal of empathy, gentleness and compassion, which is important in helping Complex Trauma sufferers to heal faster.

CHAPTER 13: SIGNS OF HEALING?

How do we know that patients have actually responded to the treatment of our Convergence Trauma Therapy?

Unfortunately, patients have the amazing capacity to block Trauma treatment at the beginning and with some, it is unconscious, with others, it is resistance to any treatment, due to attention seeking behaviour, and this may happen no matter how good we might be as a Clinician, a therapist, or as any other professional.

However, having said that, I firmly believe we do have experience and we do have ways to get past many of these resistance problems, in terms of their fears, defence mechanisms and the way a patient is acting out in the therapy room, therefore, once a patient has been 'read well' by the psychotherapist, or clinician, and a therapeutic alliance has been created, then treatment usually takes place exponentially.

The signs vary in different people and the way we react in general to anything that we deal with in life. There are many coping mechanisms we have built up over the years, so older people usually are more guarded (with the past in War time; things that are still painful and perhaps they cannot talk about it even today) with Traumas often having been entrenched in their psyche for so long, it becomes more painful to dredge them up at last, elders are often harder to work, because of their experiences in life, so generally they are often more sceptical, as they feel that "they have been there, done that, and bought the 'T' shirt!".

Young people that may have suffered abuse (especially the young teens) are often quite nervous and shy and if there has been sexual abuse, it will often cause difficulties to relax with a male or even a female therapist, dependent upon the sex of the abuser, for obvious reasons.

We are aware of these problems, so we may offer a therapist - clinician of the opposite sex, any one of whom, are trained and ready, within our practice, for that precise occasion; to help the patient with their internal pressures and hopefully encourage them to begin to feel more relaxed. We therefore have both men and women, trained to give Trauma treatment, at every level.

The signs that show how effective we have been as therapists, will vary from patient to patient and we look for these signs, even though some are so conservative or introverted and shy that we cannot always tell, until we get feedback later, either through direct spoken feedback, or the use of forms, or in some cases through their grateful family members, or friends.

Most patients immediately show relief on their faces. At first in many patients the after-affect appears to be much like bewilderment, and they may wonder, how on earth you resolved the issues so easily and quickly, as they try to work out, what just happened? That appears to most patient's, like an astonishing mystery, in the way it has suddenly healed them. Simply modern miracles, eh?

In some, you often see the patient becoming overwhelmed with joy and a great big beaming smile surfaces above the initial nervous gloom which was on their face when they first entered.

Other patients suddenly appear to be yawning with tiredness and some even realise their complete exhaustion having carried their burdens and suffering for so long.

Other patients appear to be relieved and at the same time invigorated and full of life, and look forward to live again. Others may be just tearful.

Other patients are yet so grateful and feel a bonding with you in a new closeness, because there are strange feelings that you have psychologically put them back together again, just like the nursery rhyme, of Humpty Dumpty; in that you have been through some vast experience with them in the treatment session, or even sessions over time.

Other patients appear to have more information and specific details come to mind from within the Trauma dealt with and then suddenly had surfaced within the therapy treatment, these were details which were previously hidden from their cognitive minds. In this instance memories at the time of the Trauma can become clearer momentarily, but the trapped shock and energy is released and the memories then may begin to fade also. We shall talk more on this aspect later.

And still, yet others, begin to get in touch with their anger afterwards because they felt that they had been left to suffer by the GP or the Psychiatrists or the NHS in general; because they could have accessed this treatment perhaps many years previously and found relief and a new life so easily in this new Convergence Trauma Therapy.

Tom

A patient, Tom was attending a psychiatrist once a month under a care team and on anti-depressant tablets because he had experienced a mental breakdown with psychosis and suffered separation from his wife for a couple of years.

Tom was suffering complex PTSD. The Traumas were experienced over a four year period, at the hands of a wider family member that he was staying with, while his mother needed to work elsewhere.

The Traumas were primarily of a sexual nature and the toxic shame associated with the abuse. These were perpetrated by the same elder family member who was supposed to be taking care of Tom when he stayed with their family; along with the other members of the paedophile ring, which happened when he was a child of nine years going forward.

Once the Traumas were dealt with at the mature age of 55, Tom was essentially set free from Trauma energy after only four months of treatment and him and his wife were able to begin to rebuild their lives, he was an executive director of a company and travelling worldwide, and he was now able to discuss the past in more detail in therapy more easily and had some sense of peace and life began to return to a healthier position.

The fact that Tom had not completely recovered his trust and there were still other issues we could have tackled over the long term that were, in my opinion, in need of attention but Tom decided to get on with it and step forward into what he felt was, the light at the end of that old and very long tunnel.

In this instance his wife was really happy with our work due to the change in her husband, yet on the other hand became furious when she thought about the fact that this treatment was not recognised or offered to them through the NHS after so many years of suffering.

She had not known that this treatment was even possible until a student in our College explained what we could do.

So it was infuriating, when his wife thought about this situation, all along she had not been offered, or had even been told about our modern treatments for PTSD, which would have such a dramatic and lasting effect on her husband, because their lives could have been so different, if they had known earlier.

CHAPTER 14:
TRAUMA & FEAR

Usually something really terrible has happened to a patient, in their subjective experience, that has caused the trauma and the person felt fear, as the Trauma unfolded, the Trauma was then trapped in the Amygdala in fight or flight mode.

However, in some cases there is also a great deal of fear to revisit the Trauma experience, which may initially stop the sufferer finding the help they need, as they believe that they will need to regurgitate the terrific traumatic experience and to re-visit those old skeletons in the closet. The feelings that surface seem to come upon them at times, like a tsunami of fear and foreboding, that there is something terrible lurking in there, to either hurt or haunt them again, or worse, both.

Many find that they cannot even think too much about the earlier traumas, let alone discuss them at all. This conjures up the idea that the 'boogeyman' is coming out, so we dare not go near to those buried tombs, seemingly full of dead men's bones, like revisiting old 'Davy Jones' locker, of bad, sad memories.

The other thought that comes to mind, is that if, as a sufferer, you allow yourselves to explore this old material, you will really fall apart and not be able to cope and hold everything together. There is a sense, in wanting to wait, until I am in a good place and have got stuff organised, for a period of down time, which can also be soul destroying, just existing, while waiting for a better day. Or for some, they might consider; maybe I will have a nervous breakdown, because it will take a long time and I won't be able to put Jack back in the box!

CHAPTER 15:
MENTAL ILLNESS

New research shows that many who have been wrongly assessed and given various labels or diagnosed with variations of DSM *Psychotic Disorders* when in reality they were wrongly assessed in the first place and continue to be so, when the real problem, in many cases still a problem today, is consistent with early **Trauma** and possibly complex Trauma PTSD suffered previously, quite often within very early life timescales.

There are too many pointers now to say that it is high time that those professionals in authority and those who make these psychological assessments, begin to take notice of the genuine research by Universities and the feedback from many independent therapists. Therefore, it is our firm belief that so much of severe mental illness is caused by Trauma.

It is quite sad to see so many patients coming to us having been given these labels that have quite frankly changed their lives and those around them as they have often become a dumping ground because of the attitudes towards them once they have been given a label of Borderline which today so many more people (due to the internet information explosion) are cognoscente with many terms which are still given to patients that carry so much stigma for them.

These incorrectly diagnosed people have to carry this burden around daily whenever they try to give reason for the way they are acting or just when completing application forms, etc, suddenly the toxic shame is felt and these poor unfortunate sufferers are then held accountable as a lame excuse for the butt and blame of many problems and this is not necessarily so.

It is easy to see that any conflict or disagreement may be easily put down to another party's 'personality disorder'. It is very convenient and although there are times when those who are correctly diagnosed are problematic due to their unconscious acting out, we should still not use the labels to excuse our own wrong behaviours when dealing with these people. It is no wonder that these sufferers are subject to fearful or furious rejection reactions and often witness a partisan attitude from their carer(s).

If we know that there are so many wrong diagnosis problems then we have got to be aware and look for the signs of Trauma earlier and certainly before anyone is labelled. I am hoping this book will act as a guide in training others to look for the signs in counselling, therapy or the other caring professions, so that professionals may easier spot the signs of stress and early Trauma in the acting out and the root causes pointing to adult behaviors in the present.

One wonders how many young people have been incarcerated because they were troublesome or disenfranchised, perhaps been closed off from family life, or in many institutions; perhaps been in and out of foster homes due to problems of misdiagnosis of adolescents? And being written off, as worthless, hopeless, psychotic, or just plain crazy, etc.

Some clinicians believe the term borderline personality disorder ought to be done away with altogether now, because it is seen to be so prejudicial, just like hysteria was and that too was scrapped.

Apparently three types of troublesome diagnosis have often been applied to survivors of the many childhood abuses. *Somatization Disorder, Borderline Personality Disorder,* and *Multiple Personality Disorder.* If we go back a few years these patients were simply tagged under the obsolete term '*hysteria*'.

How often, have sufferers been wrongly diagnosed, when presenting the symptoms of relationship problems and intimacy issues, or co-dependency responses to others needs and the sad tendency to become victimised throughout their lives.

Unsurprisingly due to the aforesaid tick box conveyor belt mentality of many modern trained clinicians, the direct link with major Trauma has not been picked up; which has taken the psychoanalysis completely in the wrong direction and not-withstanding the problem that the clinicians have not been trained in Complex Trauma therapy.

Robert

One of my clients named Robert, was treated with specialist Trauma therapy over several months at our clinic and in that time we dealt with many extreme Traumas inflicted upon the patient, as a young autistic child, in that time. This is where violence between mother and father had caused so many fears and problems to someone who was also obviously well inside the autistic spectrum and the father also appeared to be on the autistic spectrum disorder (ASD).

Yet he was not only diagnosed with a personality disorder because he was not conforming well to the treatment plans and directions of the 'team' there was no mention of traumas or autism in the report given.

Indeed it was only my interventions with major Trauma work over a protracted time and the patient's independent autism assessment that recorded him high enough to get plenty of help started to show signs of much less stress due to the patient self-awareness and general understanding which therefore improved his quality of life.

Yippee, It has suddenly transpired, that the personality disorder has now been reassessed as part of his autism and his consequential sensitivity. At last, a decent and sensible diagnosis and I was right all the time!

CHAPTER 16: CONVERGENCE TREATMENTS

This is the opportunity offered to our Trauma patients. When we work with patients we are aware that these Traumas are very real and very disturbing. Therefore we always work on making the therapy as gentle as possible.

Much of sexual abuse Trauma brings isolation, there is the untold secret that cannot be understood by the way abuse has affected the patient personally and individually.

One of the major contributions to feeling loved is being accepted without judgement and being able to find someone (therapist or clinician) whom the patient feels has a commonality in understanding, where the therapist may self-disclose also having suffered abuse and survived.

This is a dynamic within group work with other survivors and is refreshing to the patient and why it can be very therapeutic and brings the sense of belonging and relief because they really can understand me and relate properly to what the patient has been through too, so there is a real awareness at a deeper level of feelings without having to explain all the effects which may be overwhelming.

Patients who have had childhood abuse will often be totally ashamed to even brooch the subject with anyone and it will often only come to light as an adult when the questions of life and existence become more prominent in the person's life and usually when they begin to have children of their own.

There is often shame and guilt involved in these type of Traumas which will need to be tackled after the Trauma and not before. At the same time there is often, divided loyalties, to other close parties, which may be causing further disturbance in the patient, strategically if the perpetrator is a family member.

The idea of asking a patient to explain what the abuse was all about is not a good idea initially as it is often too painful and Trauma is right there to resurface at any moment. In these instances we would teach the patient to find some relaxation and meditation before we tackle the longer term abuse. The question is often asked how can you deal with a few Traumas and expect it to fix all the years of Trauma quickly. The fact is there are no guarantees to any therapy.

However, we know by experience that the vast majority of Trauma problems being suffered follow a usual journey of process in therapy the way we work here. The idea is to calm the patient and teach them ways to reduce anxiety while we work towards the first Trauma.

We then begin by tackling the worst of the Traumas first with our stage one CET therapy where our clinicians (excuse the metaphor) begin by cutting the tops off the 'mountains of Trauma land' and later in stage two then we begin to deal with the sludge in the bottom of the valleys in between.

Sometimes sufferers of complex Trauma / PTSD ask clinicians, "How on earth do you find the worst Traumas?". Well, as you might imagine, we do have specific ways that have been worked out to help any patient find out in detail which Traumas are the most significant ones or perhaps the most severe.

For that purpose we have a questionnaire that has been designed to help the patient collect and then funnel their Traumas and their affect into an impacting decision making tool we can use to target the right areas quickly.

CHAPTER 17: SPIRITUALITY & TRAUMA

The spiritual dimension to Trauma and recovery?

Complex trauma survivors often experience a spiritual crisis with a loss of faith. When considering Spirituality in regards to Trauma, is it really a loss of faith, or pure Ignorance.

This can be more about the sufferer's 'philosophy of relationship' rather than a spiritual crisis and particularly where Trauma may often cause a changed world view of people, even deity, or in some cases, it may be about the world (people generally) not being good enough, or even about the frustration of encroaching religion, rather than true spirituality which would normally be accompanied by a sense of transcendence and/or renewal.

Or for those who may have developed a sense of faith, it can develop into a loss of faith, regarding how they feel about themselves; furthermore it can also promote a loss of faith, in the self.

This is why many complex trauma survivors walk away from their religious beliefs, but not so prevalent for those having a very deep spiritual relationship to God with corresponding heart attitude changes, instead of a purely mental assent to a religious lifestyle or an attitude of religiosity.

For example, with some sufferers, those who have been led wrongly to believe, in a made up, spiritual 'Higher Being' and not the actual 'Creator of the Universe' shown in the Bible, whom we are taught, is both 'Loving and Compassionate' on the one hand (God is... Love) and also both 'True and Just' on the other hand and expects to call everyone to account one day.

Now obviously, without the full understanding and enlightenment that spiritual awareness brings through discernment of the spiritual dimensions. This is usually gleaned through revelation in studies of the ancient texts, and the perceived knowledge that this God will indeed exact justice for all of our actions.

It seems we cannot believe in a perfect Higher Being (God) who appears to the ignorant, to be suffering a sort of bi-polar disorder. Therefore, when it comes to the abuser's evil behaviour, sufferers may well be offended by such disgraceful actions and without wisdom, may then deduce, if God condones evil by letting evil things happen; then surely He must be evil, so they feel justified to come to this conclusions.

How can a just God let guilty sinners go free? Contrary to popular atheistic belief, we learn that God actually does not allow evil to be carried out without consequences. God does keep account of all these things and the guilty will be punished. We do not need to worry about that. This is a question the Bible answers fully and to cut the story short, the good definitely triumphs over evil, in the end. Let me explain a little more.

Perhaps this suggestion, that I offer, is near to what some have been taught as children and may have been carried through to adulthood. It goes something like this. Consider 'The BFG' (Big Friendly Giant) type of Higher being, which was constructed for children's consumption, and we use this kind of descriptive way of viewing God, to protect children's vulnerable little minds, so they would not be afraid of this Higher Being.

This would mean we are not called to account at all, because someone has unwittingly constructed a picture (not unlike Father Christmas) of this gentle old man, presumably dressed in white, with a big white beard, sat on a big fluffy white cloud and smiling down at us all the time, without any obedience required or any discipline metered out for anything and where this gentle old man called God, is being tolerant of every evil thing this world wants to do to one another; because He is the totality of political correctness and is therefore tolerant beyond measure, unless of course he stepped on any minority groups.

Or the other novel idea, sold to many when young, is of this gentle Jesus, meek and mild, who is always smiling, and accepting bad things being done, even to Him and forgiving everyone.

But this inaccurate teaching, which is only one side of a very distorted coin, peddled by the ignorant do-gooder's for their own agenda's and who are usually hypocritical, like us all, and these types cannot tolerate accountability to any higher moral standard of reference, namely God and where these champions of tolerance have essentially sown bad seed; we need to begin to address.

Unfortunately this false teaching of the things of God has had a dramatic affect on many sufferers that are ill informed. At the same time, the Trauma sufferer is often told by ignorant people that this God allows suffering and heinous abuse to occur.

This of course is considered without the fuller understanding, and that is, we are all given a choice in this world; either to be good or evil and we cannot blame this Higher Being, when we are following evil ways. Essentially it is where we humans, are the ones to mess up and do bad things to others, it is a strange idea that we blame a Higher Being (God) for the acts of malicious people intent on doing evil. The damaged abusers, the greedy fat cats and the blatantly violent perpetrators of rape and such like, including those who are tempted to do all manner of evil things, must surely take personal responsibility for that.

We have lost our moral compass and the world is not becoming a better place, just look around you. This is why we need the Law courts to combat this evil in society. But for those who have been sold a lie to blame God, this can feel like the ultimate betrayal. This is something needing considerable compassion and we need to help these sufferers and this is where the Convergence Psycho-Spiritual model comes into its own, as we uncover these feelings of betrayal and guilt trips placed on them by religion and dogma, so what they see is a damaging spirit of hypocrisy and lies, but where in reality, there is love, peace and acceptance.

My other new book, due to be published in October 2019, explains the reality of your unique soul qualities from a purely simple spiritual perspective and is called, '**Your Soul Nature Is Love**' *The Convergence Psycho-Spiritual Model in action'*. BOOTY'S NOTES series of publications published through Amazon.

CHAPTER 18: DON'T SUFFER IN SILENCE

There really is a great light at the end of the tunnel for Trauma sufferers! Surely its all about hope that something can be done for the poor sufferers of this debilitating Trauma problem. I am very sure we can offer relief to Trauma victims. I saw a sign in a shop window in a place called Horsham some while ago that tickled my humor, but I will also bring it up to date somewhat;

"Due to economic reasons, while waiting for Brexit, and the Covid plandemic to gain herd immunity, the light at the end of the tunnel has unfortunately been switched off".

We need to give suffering Trauma patients hope and that there is help at the end of their tunnel of suffering. Things have changed a lot in this area of Traumatology and the related neuroscience and researched material being utilised. I imagine Trauma work today could be likened to what surgery was like in medieval times without modern anesthetic and how today surgery can be relatively painless with modern advancements.

A doctor (anesthetist) friend of mine explained that trainee anesthetists in hospital should rarely see a patient die on the table, because of the modern advancements in anesthetic medication with comprehensive training and equipment to keep them alive, but the problem of death is more likely when the patients are in recovery and pull tubes out or discharge themselves from hospital and when they are back functioning on their own vital organs. I trust it is comforting to know that we are not going to lose anyone in Trauma therapy and we are able to contain their suffering when they are sufficiently primed beforehand.

We are able to ease the Trauma suffering and the patient goes on a healing journey as a process, even though it can be uncomfortable for a while, it is possible to stay positive as there are advantages immediately if the patient co-operates with our trained clinicians.

There are other great Trauma professionals out there, that I know too, just like us with a heart to ease suffering and that may help to really deal with the Traumas and not just offer to talk about it and perhaps re-traumatise the person.

We offer a place where you can stop the Trauma in its tracks, once and for all, and gain a better way of life free from terrible Trauma symptoms.

What irritates me a great deal in this work is to know that there are many people being fobbed off and sufferers are often told they need to get some counselling. It may be a surprise to those in the NHS, but listen up, CBT does not fix everything and for many it fixes nothing at all. When these Trauma patients need proper professional Therapy don't try to fob them off with CBT please.

The person needs to get themselves to a Trauma Specialist, such as a fully trained over at least 4 years, that has graduated, qualified and working regularly as a psychotherapist with psychotherapist supervision; It is far more advantageous in the long run and the professional might be named as a psychotraumatologist, or psychotraumatist.

Here in Convergence we specialise in training mature psychotherapy graduates to become clinicians in psychological Trauma and will use many different techniques with different patients to heal the person of this debilitating Trauma affect. One size does not fit everyone so we do need a good comprehensive tool kit in Integrative psychotherapy.

CHAPTER 19: WHAT IS GOING WRONG?

Difficulties – Science or Craft?

For a start there is the problem we face with the training levels that differentiate psychotherapists from counsellors, yet this is not acknowledged widely enough right now. And in my opinion being wrongly herded as counsellors and psychotherapists under the same label therefore causes the majority to incorrectly believe that we are all at the same level of competence within our profession, which is quite ludicrous.

There are similarities between counselling and psychotherapy, yes, of course to become a psychotherapist we must master the counselling role model and learn to deal with listening skills and everything else that is taught in basic counselling.

With psychotherapy, we realise too that the medical model is there too, as we need to study psychiatric levels of mental health issues in patients and learn about prescription drugs and the recreational drugs, but there are more skills and craft orientated work so psychotherapy also becomes an art even though some may gain Masters of 'Science'.

There are those who rightly also defend the Masters of 'Art' in psychotherapy with involved emotional relational skills along with the psychology subject matter, but in any case, psychotherapy has traditionally been seen to be working at a deeper level of competence as a psychotherapist rather than as a counsellor that spans a spectrum of training which could be literally, as a simple counsellor who may be very ill-informed or an advanced counsellor with greater skills they have added that is advanced trained up to a 'psychotherapeutic' counsellor, but nevertheless, it does matter to those of us who know the difference and definition between the two should be stated.

A well-known psychotherapist, was asked a pertinent question, some while back, namely, *"What is the difference between a counsellor and a psychotherapist?"* and the informed reply was, *"about £40,000 plus"*. Meaning the cost of post graduate level education for a psychotherapist including personal therapy for three years and supervised clinical client work and the fact psychotherapists are expected to work with in depth personality disorders and extreme areas of mental health sufferers; this all determines there is a real need to make this distinction between the two disciplines though similar yet distinctly different in depth of work and training.

The general level of Counsellors is at a basic undergraduate Level-4 standard diploma or level-5 higher diploma and they are not trained as psychotherapists. There are always exceptions to the rule, and yes, some have been trained at undergraduate degree level, or postgraduate Masters level but they are usually psychotherapeutic counsellors not psychotherapists.

Unfortunately, and to my knowledge, the authorities responsible for the local government run colleges of higher education (that were previously funded to teach counselling, from level-1 to level-5) did not recognise psychotherapy as an accessible level for a baseline education requirement to access mental health care. Therefore it was not at a level for higher level education but rather post graduate level; comparable to University degree levels so did not warrant funding because psychotherapy is a much higher level of training. What did they do?

Well the next thing that happened is that Universities

managed to bring 'part psychotherapy' training under the umbrella of postgraduate levels by calling it 'psychotherapeutic counselling' and made it more accessible to a growing desire by students to study counselling and so gained the needed funding at that level. Obviously this was an opportunity to those who felt they could stretch a little to learn more at a University level, training in the counselling modality they already had learned.

From a business standpoint (all organisation require cash flow to survive) I can see nothing wrong with that scenario, but unfortunately it blurs the lines for us all.

Around the time of publishing this book, the BACP launched a research debate to find out what the profession is saying about these differences and to discuss the possibilities of regulation around names and specific qualifications required to establish the lines to be drawn up.

To think that a basic level-four counsellor is able to work as a psychotherapist studying and working at a post graduate level is, quite frankly, nuts, but unfortunately that is the message being put out there by the media in not differentiating between the two and many counsellors also enjoy their pseudo-clinical status and similarly really have no idea what the difference actually is; therefore a counsellor does not realise the vast scope and levels at which a psychotherapist is experientially trained to know and see from the language and behaviours of others; including what the psychotherapist is able to accomplish, with even quite disturbed and damaged people.

When we add effective Trauma training to the qualified training in psychotherapy it enhances understanding for anyone attempting Trauma work.

Surely it is useful and reassuring for Trauma sufferers to know that their clinician is also a fully trained psychotherapist working at a deeper level. There is a lot that psychotherapists may offer in Trauma work by way of the talking cure with this deeper professional understanding of the human psyche.

The majority of Mental Health training in Universities and the in house training of all nursing and mental health teams of the NHS is primarily based on the medical model, which has historically built on either biochemical or surgical interventions for everything and anything. Therefore all training must follow this scientific route to be accepted and fit within the BMA / Psychiatric Handbooks that determine medical care. This all sounds great on the surface, but...

Within this medical model remit of doctoral training and the hospital care system generally, all treatment planning is supposed to be motivated by 'evidence' based clinical care, and this model has been used for those trained within the mental health care services in the NHS system and the acute care teams being run by psychiatrists.

Unfortunately, the scientific evidence based system has allegedly broken down at the crucial point of having little or no evidence to back up the theories put forward by the psychiatrists contributing to these psychiatric handbooks. You will find some author's books and other papers online addressing this problem of incorrect or spurious diagnosis of mental health issues that have just been decided with little or no backing up to 60% of the diagnosed issues found in the books.

So this all goes against, what we believed was scientific evidence based understanding, at the root of all training now. How are we to trust this kind of nonsense, which has purportedly been thrown together and fed into the system by those in authority, now that it has become general knowledge.

Please check it out for yourself and be ready to comment on this farcical, so called medical professionalism, as a standard by which those in the NHS judge every therapist with, and to bring this unethical behaviour into the public eye.

We need wisdom and experience to bear on this platform,

yet we also need trustworthy research and not just a team of people simply getting together to confer on certain criteria and then to decide what is crucial in accurate assessments of vulnerable patients, without the qualitative evidenced base.

In my view and the views of many other professionals that I have spoken to, suggests that a work of this importance, where this important information is also calling into being 'complex assessments' and in so doing decides a poor patient's fate, and which is only hinged on the contributing professional authors limited views, which is scandalously served up to our profession without a solid evidence base, surely this is ludicrous in this day and age.

I have also noticed much in regard to our suffering patients and the so called professional carer's as I began to recognise why the mental health care and social services are not working well in our mental health community and in society generally.

My own training was very experiential and I have now also developed a more holistic approach and a renewed focus on the uniqueness of the soul personhood and essence of the individual patient. I am concerned more with our 'relating with' rather than objectifying patients.

The NHS unfortunately offer an abstract medical method and need to organise treatment plans and therefore psychologists and many other medical professionals, for that matter, often make copy and pastes style assessments, and the Mental Health teams use convenient psychiatric labels which are now hotly debated as not even evidence based.

Surely we should start to strip away the labels and get to know who the individual is and how best to treat the person.

Also, it occurs to me just how difficult it must be for others within the National Health Service (NHS) whom are trained solely in this 'medical' model, which is usually quite a tick box method of assessment interviewing rather than really trying to see and hold the clients and to understand them at a personal level and not just to know stuff about them on a psychological level which all seems quite cold to suffering patients and other independent care givers.

I feel that essentially ineffective treatment plans are being put in place everywhere with the NHS, ignoring or worse, not even recognising Trauma issues, or issues around ASD (Autistic Spectrum Disorder) traits, in their patient's, and that these poor unfortunate souls are under these care packages in the Mental Health services system, causing enormous waiting times (currently here in Milton Keynes it's a nine month waiting list) and these blockages then exacerbate a lack of holistically real care for patients, at the end of the day.

And in so doing this often bring these so called professionals to disrespect other independent qualified and competent carers, which is done through professional jealousy, in an effort to defend their own tick box clinical directives and corresponding actions and consequences that can be, and often is, dire for their patients

Checks & Balances needed

There are many extremes and controlling elements within the caring professions and with patients in general.

It is my view that there is also a real presence of professional jealousy and growing incompetence and lack of care that is damaging patients and therapists alike.

We do need checks and balances within professional ethics and at the same time, to reach for transcendent ways to truly care for each other and recognise people as persons and not just as 'our work'. We are still facing a difficult time in this blame culture and the demand for evidence based results should be fair and not manipulated to balance the books or to just manage the numbers and let care go out of the window.

Finances have to be juggled and managers are needed but not in this top heavy management world of NHS health care. It should contain attitudes towards patients and professionals without prejudices and dump a lot of the political correctness, in this extreme faddish blame culture today (surely the latest madness within society).

CHAPTER 20: DISINTEGRATION AND PSYCHOTHERAPY

Obviously Trauma causes many problems and often we must work with the Trauma patients after we have gained a level playing field and need to work on the general psychotherapy issues that may or may not have also been affected by the trauma situation or previous / later life issues that also may affect the patient's philosophy of life, so there is a need for more in depth work at times.

It is important to realise when we are working with people that we will sometimes have to deal with heavier issues in our patient's minds. We may need to deal with a psychological disintegration; which all may sound horrific, but it is not really; we simply need to peel back the time and look at her inner child by separating out many of the layers established as templates of experience (both good and bad) that were laid down earlier in the psyche and with the help from an experienced psychotherapist we may be able to find the hurts and the relevant defence mechanisms developed in the unconscious which we have formed to protect and enable ourselves.

At the point of disintegration, we may then re-examine our intrapsychic contact, the introjects from parents and all the self-speak we do, with the processes we go through, both intra-personally and inter-personally, to perhaps find a healthier way, if there is one. This all helps you to truly find yourself and helps you put yourself back together (unlike humpty dumpty) but you are not alone anymore to and with a psychotherapist facilitating and empowering us through those so important changes we may just learn to truly live healthier and happier lives.

Where necessary we are to make appropriate interventions and this involves transference and counter-transference as something to be welcomed for the client where they may realise new positive life experiences, for example, with the therapist perhaps in the re-parenting role and where the unconscious id drives are considered and explored together by opening the patient's unconscious processing.

It could be the Oedipus or Electra complex where we may need to work with gender by exploring the anima and animus to help with a confused gender situation or specific gender attractions or LGBT issues and any difficulties requiring caring help to establish and/or find healthier options or lifestyle. It could be simply finding the right path for the individual or to make sense of life and archetypical roles.

This is where we often act out a situation in the therapy room and truly become the 'good parent' so that the patient learns what it is like to have a good parent instead of a biological natural one that was not helpful or even neglectful or even critically, physically, sexually abusive and so they eventually learn, through therapy, to self-nurture; with the therapist playing the role of the good parent and a new positive input is offered.

The client will learn new ways of being in that scenario, all of which helps where a person was perhaps intimidated or dismissed and ignored and perhaps had no voice, rather than loved and encouraged, that becomes 'grist for the mill' and therefore welcomed as a new experience for the patient in therapy, rather than to be cautioned by some police styled humanistic trainers, or supervisors, in what best could be described as neurotic counselling organisations, when they are talking (ignorantly) about what they feel is that horrid thing called 'counter transference', where students are warned about not reacting and transferring their own issues and pain back onto the patients, yet often delivered to student counsellors as some sort of evil thing without any understanding of the good you may do with your good parent transference.

No surprise that this may be taught in some places, if the students are not expected to have psychotherapy and deal with their own issues, it could contribute to fear around the problems that type of client transference may bring up in the counsellor, but not so in psychotherapy where we teach and use it to great effect. This becomes part of the psychotherapy dance, where there is also the 'mirroring' in the dance of the therapeutic alliance and congruence reigns to bring lasting change.

Some few students may opt for easier routes from the psychotherapy training after achieving basic counselling skills to a foundation level-3 which is fairly easy to learn with Convergence, but this is because we begin to go deeper through the level 3 in experiential training which is very exciting and students learn so much about themselves, as training develops.

But some find this part too challenging and decide to try further add-on style counselling courses, or go for psychology degrees, or even try forensics instead, but sadly they will never truly know what they were missing when they flunk out at this stage. And this is apparently why so few go for Gold and become Psychotherapists today and there are so many levelled off as just basic counsellors.

However, I am really pleased to report that other students who are brave enough to honestly learn about themselves and their own unconscious material grow and develop personally into skilled clinicians and often become great psychotherapists who are life-long learners and are able to really engage with people at a deeper level than most and these are the ones who empower patients and often save client's lives and their families in the process, these are my peer heroes and some go on to become tutors themselves and give something back to the profession.

The scientific diagnostic attitude

It seems the care system breaks down for patients in much of the relational work being carried out and is mainly due to this scientific diagnostic medical model and the ensuing mentality shown towards patients, in the NHS management systems, and particularly with regards to those in 'position' within these NHS services, right across the board of care, including senior managers, doctors and psychiatrists, in many of their mental health teams.

The reason this apparently happens is because each patient comes in to a tick box care assessment system (based wrongly on farcical evidence based research) within the NHS trained medium and as the medical model, which is not really a personalised model, it is quite dehumanising in much of the experience of their patients.

According to the many reports we have heard from other professionals, and both clients, or trauma patients, or individuals from our many client's and student's families using the NHS, and what we have personally witnessed with our psychotherapy and trauma patients over the last decade at least, this is the way it appears to work.

What we notice regarding breakdowns

I have also noticed much in regard to our suffering patients and the so called professional carer's as I began to recognise why the mental health care and social services are not working well in our mental health community and in society generally.

Also how difficult it must be for others within the National Health Service (NHS) whom are trained solely in this 'medical' model, which is usually quite a tick box method of assessment interviewing rather than really trying to see and hold the clients and to understand them at a personal level and not just to know stuff about them on a psychological level which all seems quite cold to suffering patients and other independent care givers.

We do not want to rely on the NHS biochemical and often outdated and harmful methods in continual drug prescriptions, which push many into addictions when it is unnecessary if a person is given trauma therapy quickly.

I feel that essentially ineffective treatment plans without recognising Trauma or those with ASD (Autistic Spectrum Disorder) traits of their patient's, under the care of the Mental Health services, which cause enormous waiting times and these blockages then determine a lack of real care to patients in the end.

And in so doing this often bring these so called professionals to disrespect other independent qualified and competent carers, which is done through professional jealousy, in an effort to defend their own tick box clinical directives and corresponding actions and consequences that can be, and often is, dire for their patients.

Drama into a crisis

From the experience reported to us by these NHS disgruntled patients and those independent professionals like myself, looking on in dismay, it is acted out dramatically something like this;

A person starts acting out some sort of breakdown, often brought on by what we recognise as trauma/s, or perhaps due to neglect or abuse or various disabilities, there is obviously a lack of coping skills and difficulties in dealing with in life in general and usually what follows is the onset of mild worries or major anxieties and the ensuing problems with sleep hygiene. And we know that sleep deprivation is a killer.

According to what I have read in Matthew Walker's

research book on sleep, we all need eight hours to stay healthy, which is a view I wholeheartedly agree with.

The patient often slips further into depression and according to other research around today showing that there is often a big link to alcohol or drug misuse causing many further problems, which is solidly in the mix around this stage, as the person tries to self-medicate to alleviate suffering, or worse, when it culminates with a psychotic breakdown and then the local mental health Intervention team will finally spring into action, or unfortunately not, in some cases.

If a person is sectioned through Police interventions if the patient is kicking off physically or doing strange things, they are usually brought in to A & E, or better still they are referred to the mental health unit where they are medicated and usually left to cook for a while.

After admission the mental health workers often operate as teams, and although professionally trained, they will often using the cheapest paid staff due to financial pressures which I will not delve into here; so they will use care assistants, mental health nurses, cpn's, or care workers, even social workers to act as go-betweens when there are issues within care teams and patients, although we find many patients are under-represented and finally give up without having a voice to address this uncaring attitude to their mental health.

There is a need to interact with these patients on a personal level, but for the majority of the time what happens is that they get patients individually assessed by a psychiatrist or psychologist where they are interviewed and at times simply get another tick box style session.

Copy & Paste with complex language for reports

Patients often report that the assessments that follow are sadly laughable at their lack of correct details, there is much' copying and pasting' that goes on in these psychological reports, even to the courts I have found.

I heard from more than one patient that the judge assessing their social case at court (whilst exploring psychologist's report) have said, "please rewrite this report without the complex jargonised language so that we can all understand what you are trying to say!".

There is usually a quick label issued for an assessment, when there is a psychiatrist available, to mainly ensure there is clarity to find out what drugs will treat that condition, and they are in the pipeline to be prescribed and that is often under wrongly diagnosed mental issues.

Unfortunately the psychiatrists and psychologists do not usually realise that independent practitioners most often show an even greater sense of a duty of care to patients in their care, than those professionals within these governmental halls. How difficult it is for many professionals within the NHS to accept that others outside of the mainline training spectrum have training in more modern and effective skills and often more flexible facilities, hours, etc, and a true sense of personhood in treatment of our patients.

Professional jealousy is also rife in these areas of professional care and although the NHS staff do a great job in many cases of care across the board throughout hospitals of which we are truly grateful, nevertheless, there is a great deal of room for improvement within mental health care platforms and policies.

Primarily in private practice, with patients, as a psychotraumatologist and with many interactions directly and indirectly with other caring professionals, I have discovered many beautiful things as a spiritual person who became a psychotherapist and firmly believe that I am a wounded healer that enjoys the satisfaction of helping others on their journey of discovery, where they are gaining a new found freedom, mainly experienced through the mandatory personal psychotherapy students must attend for personal growth and which helps us all in the profession; where we are able to look deeper into ourselves with a guiding therapist to help us.

It was this personal therapy, that was mandatory in my psychotherapy training, where I was personally able to begin to deal more with my early childhood covering areas around major critical father issues, like so many others have today. Consequently these days, I am fortunately able to nurture my inner child and find solid ground when those criticisms come from others and it is so helpful to find the liberation to simply just be me, warts and all.

My eyes have also been opened to the many difficult issues we face as independent professionals from the critics and naysayers in our communities (blame culture again) as I can now fairly objectively evaluate what can only be described, in some quarters, as professional jealousy, particularly through the NHS, with the results we are achieving here in Convergence Psychotherapy and the personal practices that have grown through it with our psychotherapy graduates.

CHAPTER 21: THE CBT SYSTEM

I am now critiquing the system, not the workers. Having seen this system in operation, for many years, we believe it is a horrific way to treat patients. Obviously, almost everyone is aware of the condition of the poor old NHS, and I want to say something positive, before criticising the way we do it here in UK.

There is a great deal of helpful and positive inputs, that many of us independent therapists, could verbally inject into the NHS system and maybe help to find ways that alleviate all this suffering, 'if only' we were allowed to have a say and contribute some fresh ideas.

The NHS are also scuppering the many well-meaning and caring, independent therapists, by thumbing the nose at the counselling profession's workforce, which they have done, by attempting to use fast track (sticky plaster) training, for their own people (nursing staff) using simple quick courses in CBT which are truly inadequate for purpose, presumably to save money, instead of tapping this great and vast workforce of fully trained people, which affects the further training, colleges and individual's right to work and to gain jobs for the many good qualified therapists.

No wonder the NHS is struggling to give proper care in this field of endeavour too. There is a considerable and vastly untapped reservoir of qualified counsellors and psychotherapists out there, and that the NHS could manage and employ, to address this problem of staff shortages and waiting times for their patient's mental health needs. And, Yes! We do need the Government and local authorities to inject some funds. And this inclusion of existing counsellors and therapists could bring newer methods in, which are also evidence based, to support the ailing mental health side of the NHS medical factory.

Then there is this other hot chestnut of labelling, around mental health diagnosis, right now, that nobody appears to want to really sort out. I have now termed this disingenuous categorical system and ongoing meaningless labelling of patients as the "NHS *'Conveyor Belt Treatment (CBT)'* system", which is their managed model of basic care in Mental Health work right now. What a shame! We do not wish to metaphorically kick a dog when it's down, but there needs to be a real shake-up of this disingenuous and abusive labelling system which causes stigma and prejudice.

Because everyone sees that it is failing and many people are suffering in mental health services because of it and particularly those suffering trauma right now and just as we recognise the drives in many hospital heart surgeons who may have this Saviour complex going on at times, in similar ways, so do the Psychiatrists and Psychologists and their care teams. They have the same overinflated sense of importance and with a misplaced sense of puffed up pride while in the process of delivering this shocking lack of continuing care to patients once the patient is at the end of their NHS conveyor belt.

This is the way it operates to those observing. In short, the patient comes in to the system in various stages of crisis, usually due to traumas, in their lives and the patient initially finds they are not coping like they used to do. Or it may be in some cases, we have heard of, that it is nothing major but simply mild mood to borderline clinical depression disturbances on the Beck scale and for whatever reason a patient is not coping with life very well. This could be due to many reasons such as marital problems, child rearing, divorce, bereavement, financial problems, redundancy, bullying, or other life crisis situations, including many childhood issues re-surfacing in the present and simply require some basic counselling support.

But for many others that are suffering trapped shock (Trauma) in the situations they have faced, and cannot seem to move forward with life. For many it has been an uncomfortable part of life for many years; but they were not aware of the fact they had some traumas that could be rectified, or were too worried to go for treatment, because they have not been informed that trauma can be resolved fairly quickly now by a Trauma specialist. There is no need to continue to suffer in silence these days. For many it has already developed, or will grow darkly, into something called full blown PTSD in the future.

I get so sad seeing the magnificent heroes in our armed forces filmed on the many documentaries where they are suffering from PTSD and complex trauma issues without relief having been sent to simple counselling often disguised as modern help for trauma, instead of specialist treatment by people who may move trauma very quickly and without much pain rather than see men and women suffering and living difficult and problematic lives and often struggling to just to cope on a day to day basis. Using distracting techniques that only work in part and fed the idea of mindfulness or the NHS answer to everything, simple trauma focused CBT which appears to prolong the agony of these poor people. When I hear the stories I just want to help them to live differently and give them hope. This is partly the reason for this book.

My Trauma therapy skills and that of my students I am in no doubt is probably the best trauma therapy in the world. I have cured sufferers in one session of a rape or violent accident or any manner of different situations, where trapped shock (trauma) is holding the person in terror, anxiety and fears. The symptoms are horrific to witness and the stories I hear would make your hair curl. Obviously it is important to look after oneself in this work too.

The patient then goes through their GP, is assessed and given Anti-depressants prescriptions are in many instances wrong treatments for people who are suffering from worry that are often in normal sadness and grief, or even those who may experience mild mood to severe depressive disturbances, as anti-depressants are now being recognised more fully as a drug to mask feelings and may be an aid to slow the mind down.

These pills are often prescribed to mask physical pain as well, which indirectly is supposed to help with depression, but unfortunately we see that many are being pushed into addiction, when it is really unnecessary where the person is given help to work through their worries and emotions in therapy and with specialist trauma therapy to gain help fast, rather than having to wait around for the NHS style quick course of CBT, on the what? Yes! the *'Conveyor Belt Treatment'* system.

So the patient on drugs often says, I feel down and think I want to just end it all and the GP panics and puts the patient on some so called anti-depressant pills and then later, without proper effective therapy, the patient eventually goes into melt down when problems worsen. The patient gets a referral and is assessed and labelled by a psychiatrist accordingly; let's say labelled as 'Borderline Personality Disorder', just for an example. The patient gets further or different meds due to their new assessment.

Trauma is neither diagnosed or even exposed and certainly not dealt with at this stage, usually because the psych has not picked it up in the discussions. To be fair, with many chaotic clients it may be hard to get clear indications whilst they are in a manic phase, so assessments are fraught with variables at the stage of admission. And we realise trauma specialisation as therapy care or training to offer it costs money and the NHS cuts mean finances are not there to help, so it is no surprise that current waiting time is up to 18 months in Milton Keynes for the NHS standard for trauma therapy, which is EMDR if you are offered it – it is more expensive to access, because of the specialised nature of the work within psycho-traumatology.

The patient is then usually put into some sort of agreed treatment plan by the psychologist and team. The patient is pushed towards agreement here and all sorts of bribery and manipulations happen at this point, around housing, benefits, etc, to get patients to move along the conveyor belt and all in good NHS time, it does not seem to matter how the patient feels at this point often of despair.

The next phase is usually where the patient is allocated to a care team who initially offer some social care and other or more medication and patient is sent on their way (under the supervised eye of the department allocated at the time) or given sheltered housing through an charitable organisation and this is where it often goes wrong again, because some care teams systematically dehumanise the patient, and patent's often find they are not listened to, care workers in the various teams (who have not had therapy themselves) are often acting out their own personal self-worth and control issues which happens across the board and goes unchecked in the caring professions, hardly surprising that this is happening as these so called 'carers' have had 'no personal therapy' themselves. Just look at the abuses going on in care homes and with vulnerable adult homes that panorama has shown up recently, it is shocking to the general public but not to ourselves.

Once the patient has been given a label this makes life easier for those in charge because everything may then be associated with the fact the client is difficult due to their label /disorder, so little need to listen to them now.

I can almost hear the team leader in the mental Health team counting off and saying, almost at the end of the conveyor belt now... Let's see where we are with this patient now?

1). Tranquilised - check,

2). Support worker / basic counsellor – check,

3). Labelled – check,

4). Updated Meds – check.

5). Introduced to support groups – check,

6). Try to get patient to lead others in groups – check.

7). Housed temporarily – check.

8). Support withdrawn for counselling
but highly medicated – check.

9). Treatment plan in operation – check.

10). Self-responsible housed – check.

11). Leave to own devices – check.

12). Complete success patient delivered to end of belt – check.

13). Unlucky for some – patient still has all the issues,
but now has been through our system and clinically
cared for (regardless of the outcome) so there is no
need to worry about the patient from now on, we have
done what we needed to do, as our treatment plan has
covered it all and *there is the evidence base.* – **check!**

Prognosis: Patient is still with all their issues and now a
few more caused by labelling and the frustration of the
NHS professionals not listening (using the disingenuous
categorical DSM Manuals) even though they are
medicated and alive, they are far from well and usually
not functioning well on the medications and the feelings
of not being heard and not being seen and certainly
not being truly cared for hold long afterwards.

Some of these conveyor belt mental health patients still
have all their traumas (possibly PTSD) and are not coping and
hopefully will not have too many periodical melt-downs
and psychotic episodes, where the intervention team will
need to make that call again and put the patient back on the
conveyor belt and start it all over again. God help us all.

Sometimes, all that was needed was someone to pick up on the adverse life issues and / or Trauma(s) where they may be given therapy and that would have broken the cycle. We have the latest cures. We do not need to let people suffer; we just need to listen properly and really care to give a different outcome.

The Case History of Thomas

Thomas was a trauma patient who was getting nowhere with the NHS Mental Health - *Conveyor Belt Treatment* (CBT) system and whilst in a state of despair contacted us personally; initially for a psychotherapy assessment, regarding his presenting life issues, that the NHS (he felt) seemed to be largely ignoring and his neurosis appeared to be around; anxiety, nervousness, the lack of confidence and depression. Thomas attended my offices within about ten days.

Once in therapy, I discovered that there were two things which were fundamentally causing issues, and worse, continued to be unrecognised and therefore undiagnosed. The first was fairly obvious, the patient was very scared and highly anxious, and not coping well at all, hyper vigilance, avoidance and intrusion affect, was clearly in plain view with this person and on examination was found to have complex PTSD.

The second issue that was not quite so obvious, but became quite evident in subsequent sessions, was that the patient who was quite highly intelligent, yet was firmly within the scale of Autism.

The notion that Thomas was on the autistic spectrum disorder (ASD) scale was previously diagnosed in earlier counselling sessions, by an experienced female counsellor, who sent a letter in to Thomas's GP, for a referral, and whom the GP had totally ignored her courteous letter and then later the NHS care team had got involved when the client was sectioned eventually.

The complex PTSD issues (not helped by ASD) were going back to childhood times, incurred by vicarious trauma with parental fighting with ensuing bloody violence, which also included some rough treatment towards the patient at times to embed the traumas and cause flashbacks and nightmares and extreme hyper-arousal and much social avoidance.

The main Trauma energies were dealt with over some six months or so and the patient was making great progress. The patient was still with the care team and it was suspect that particular workers were often bullying and manipulating the patient a great deal and did not like the intervention of another professional, whom we might mention, was making marvellous improvements with their patient and the attending psychologist wanted to know what the therapist was doing exactly.

The therapist and patient realised that there was manipulation going on from the care team to hustle the patient along their tick box conveyor belt, and it was obvious that the psychologist was upset by the situation, although hard to imagine, was possibly jealous of the good work, so the patient and therapist decided to keep their confidentiality boundaries strong and when contacted the carer arrogantly demanded we proffer up a written report to their NHS team, we rightly refused on the basis of confidentiality and the fact they were questioning our validity and status and were not offering o work with us or to pay for any reporting on our work as there was no contract between us.

Unfortunately the NHS psychologist thought this was wrong in some way and complained, in a letter, to the department the patient was being transferred to; as the psychologist was leaving the area after her three month's work with the patient. It's not uncommon for their patients also to be pulled from pillar to post with psychologists continually jumping ship, for more money, in this drowning sea of Mental Health care in the NHS with this uncaring so called 'care package' being offered.

The patient had improved immensely. But then we had an unfortunate intervention by the NHS team once more a new treatment plan would be drawn up.

The prescription drugs (anti-psychotics) were being withdrawn (initially at the patient's request, because of improved health) but although the patient (and I) requested the withdrawal of drugs to be sensitively withdrawn (slowly), this was largely ignored.

The patient was being taken off of the drugs far too fast, according to pure common sense, yet although the patient reiterated this request to the newly promoted prescribing team involved, the patient became nervy and worried.

Therefore, due to the withdrawal of medication far too fast, which caused some of the traumas we worked on previously, that were partially masked by the previous drugs, then started to surface and the patient suffered a mild panic attack; with some old fears attending once more. This fortunately happened whilst back in supportive therapy and the patient was directed to go straight to A & E to get some immediate and basic medication support, just to alleviate this problem, while upset currently.

It is sad and unfortunate, that the patient was fearfully impatient, through old ghostly emotions and therefore being very scared and insecure, with no medication support at this point having been taken off the powerful drugs completely at this stage.

The patient, fearing he would fall apart, then asked his psyche team to prescribe with urgency, for his anxiety and they unfortunately changed his medication completely to some powerful drugs that caused immediate hallucinations and caused an attack of psychosis that went on for months, whilst they continued to insist on the patient taking these tablets, which they would not change.

The patient was seeing things crawling out of his body, by this stage and quite desperate, and unbeknown to the care team and the sheltered housing staff, the patient was resorting to major alcohol and self-medication with recreational drugs, easily obtained from other patients with a lot of freedom to operate outside.

The patient then not surprisingly suffered another psychotic episode. Unfortunately, the care team then had a knee jerk reaction and put the client on different pills altogether and the patient then became quite psychotic with the effect of the new drugs and went downhill, for a further year when he began to resurface once more.

Eventually the client was put on lower doses of drugs over the next year or more and eventually went back to therapy which he trusted more than anyone.

To make matters worse, as far as the NHS care is concerned, the psychotraumatologist had diagnosed the patient with PTSD and Autism fairly early on in therapy.

The Autism was confirmed later and the trauma therapy work took place and delivered the patient of 95% of their traumas at the time (though it was already spoken of the fact that trauma may return up to 50% if the patient is on medication, whilst the trauma work is carried out) and the patient was no longer suffering PTSD.

It was then that the official Autism assessment took place and the Autistic Spectrum Disorder scale was confirmed, conclusively in the patient, as expected.

But the psychiatrist made a very wrong call, as a diagnosis whilst the patient was dealing with the badly prescribed meds and the subsequent melt-down without recognising autistic traits and difficulty issues, diagnosed the patient at that time with an specific Borderline Disorder without taking into account the PTSD issues and Autism assessment. Enough said.

As I sad previously keep us informed of your accounts within mental health circles as we need to address these issues for sufferers and highlight their needs and the holes in the UK's specialist care and to offer the NHS some feedback.

The so called 'Evidence based' NHS care in the mental health services also needs evidence presented with regards to where the current system has been going wrong as well, or we will never know about problems that require fixing.

CHAPTER 22: EFFECTIVE TRAUMA TRAINING

I wish to point out something that those within the NHS ought to listen to, namely, those in mental health care management teams, particularly the Doctors, Psychiatrists, Psychologists, psychiatric nurses, care workers and other psychotherapists within these care teams. They are peddling this outdated and dangerous method as a so called 'treatment plan' for mental health issues. It does not work well, because the Medical model in mental health has drawbacks.

It is still a joke to psychotherapists, knowing what has been brought up in training and what we have had to engage with, under personal therapy, that the vast majority of those in the Mental Health assessing seat, have not had any psychotherapy themselves; where they need to deal with so many issues, the mind boggles at the amount and depth of issues we find, unconscious issues and defence mechanisms derived from previous introjections or suffering in their young lives generally (there are no perfect parents) that is being acted out as the unconscious shadow without them even realising it. Some people in these positions within the NHS care system are quite mercenary to say the least.

Counsellors, nowadays have to have personal counselling as part of their recognised training, usually about 40-60 hours over a two year period, depending on the training institutions requirements, this is a safeguard for both the counsellor and their eventual counsellees, to ensure personal upsets are at least given opportunity to surface whilst in training; to be dealt with in personal counselling.

Psychotherapists also have personal psychotherapy as part of their training, rather than simple counselling, but this is also required as a longer term process usually on most Master's degrees, it will be covering 150 hours of personal therapy, whilst in training, so if this is important for psychotherapists to attend psychotherapy and even basic counsellors need to have some simple personal counselling.

Why then, do we not see this happening in the medical profession for mental health workers, surely the NHS are aware of this whole in training for those in the medical model or are they somehow seen to be above having some personal issues? (seems unusual with the amount of Doctors, Psychiatrists, Psychologists and various psychiatric mental health workers and carers, this list includes social workers and police officers at all levels (often with major control issues).

How many have been eventually caught up in police investigations, and subsequent court actions and even jail sentences, in just this past decade? These medics and workers have been shown to be not only a bit ego fragile, but in some cases were quite mentally unstable and some reportedly even killed people and could even be psychopaths, masked as care workers. Is there any real and worthwhile psychological testing?

Yet there is still this problem with a general lack of care, by not ensuring all doctors and mental health workers in our caring professions do undergo compulsory therapy, ensuring a holistic training, to include checks and balances on their own mental health and to be concerned for and to assess their personal growth and mental state, a subject which is blaringly obvious to those of us who know, and at the same time, the NHS insists that the medical profession have high evidence based standards to be met, meaning their doctors and nurses care.

Who gives psychotherapy to the professionals?

My question then, is this. Why is this not happening for the medical profession in the same way as the independent mental health counselling and psychotherapy professions, if these medics are to be let loose on the general public for patient care, often having to attend to mental health patients too with only a smattering of understanding and just their prescription pen ready to fix all with chemicals. Clinical supervision is not therapy! Therapy and Supervision although have some similarities, nevertheless they are very different.

To recognise that psychologists and psychiatric nurses and social workers who are looking after people suffering from mental health issues and yet these professional carers are not required to have personal psychotherapy is ridiculous in these current days of factually informed (so called) 'evidence based' standards of work, although some psychologists are 'encouraged' to have some counselling and must have 'supervision' (not therapy and often not independent) within their work as it is usually performed by other senior psychiatrists or psychologists (who also have had 'no required personal therapy' to deal with their own unconscious acting out form any and all early life issues and neither to be called to account for their shadow actions and behaviours, which we incorporate in therapy as we deal with so much shadow transference work and in our mirroring process.

Because this psychology training has little experiential work at grass roots level, of care for a person, which is born out of personal experiences in therapy; whereas in psychotherapy training often issues surface as we engage with the tutor's material delivered in a lecture or small group discussion, or as a student in one-to-one peer counselling under supervision. Psychotherapy students are usually told by the tutors and training supervisors to reflect and take what we learn on the course (especially anything we find unsettling or confusing in our own emotional make-up) to discuss in personal therapy, whereas the medical model psychology training tends to promote an unrelated clinical tick box attitude, which is totally different in mental appreciation to that of a well-trained psychotherapist.

In psychotherapy training therapy usually goes much deeper into a person's issues and for an example, on the one hand tends to bring out the patient's potential, and on the other hand often uncovers personal inner conflicts, behaviour patterns of bi-polar, and many problem areas, such as passive aggressive, or uncontrollable explosive anger, and other issues like covert narcissism or extreme avoidance due to major self-worth issues and fear. We have met many trainee doctors and those doctors in practice today, who really need therapy to resolve many issues from childhood.

There are many scenarios played out by students in the classroom using gestalt work in psychodrama and transactional analysis and other fitting therapies utilised as ways to find resolutions to the games we all play, in defending ourselves, or getting the attention we need and finding resolutions and often life changing revelation and breakthroughs surface, making us healthier human beings.

The unconscious is explored together in personal therapy when the classroom gets too invasive and we need more help to deal with hurts or wounds and to understand ourselves and the hidden true self within the shadow of the false self.

Although we find this experiential training often brings resolve to many issues right there in class perhaps with group or the supervised peer therapy that takes place right there in the classroom sometimes, or when a student personally finds that 'Aha' moment all for themselves, which is discovered as we learn together and uncover many areas of early wounding.

We really do need to have psychotherapy and not just counselling, because psychotherapy has much more in depth training and we usually have many more tools in our bag. Psychotherapists need to learn and develop more experiential skills and insight as they are trained to a deeper experiential level of knowledge; and that enables them to challenge patients and make more accurate in depth interventions, yet psychotherapists are still trained to do this from the same sensitive, gentle, but engaging and caring position.

Therefore, psychotherapy students need to realise that our work in this profession is not just gaining head knowledge alone, our courses are not purely academic (sadly that is what motivates some to study at the start to gain head knowledge) as we notice that some students begin this training full of fears (unconsciously, in some cases but not all) so that they might learn about what people are thinking and why they act in certain ways, for some students it is in order to help the student gain power over others, with partners or potential partners in particular. Obviously, this can be problematic and as tutors we need to see students grow personally and are able to apply what they learn and not just make mental notes in their head, or be able to understand enough information to simply tick boxes, but instead to experience the psychotherapy first hand and to know what it feels like to be helped.

Some just have real control issues that are usually born out of fears, this is where the student may have a felt need to just feel safer by hoping to know what is in another's mind, or simply by being able to control their own environment, which may even spill out into attempting to control friends, or even clients. This type of an only academia-style student tries to learn all the theories quickly and wants to apply to others, but does not necessarily want to change personally.

The main problem here, is the student believes that they are perfectly attuned and consider they know themselves very well, when in fact, they know little about their internal dialogue and unconscious drives (some even suffer covert narcissistic styles that are underlying even a depressive presentation) and some may find it hard to engage with the psychological material subjectively and of the many experiences provided on psychotherapy courses, for fear of being uncovered, or the prospect of experiencing failure in some way.

The dear old BACP are trying their best to make a difference, by opening dialogue with the NHS, the authorities and other chosen membership bodies, but this is somewhat of a distraction and those in authority are drawn away from, some of the more serious underlying issues, around support and fair play towards all of its members, and in so doing, unfortunately, seem to contribute to the problem rather than the solution.

Let me explain what I feel has gone wrong in the BACP's role and rule, primarily towards representation of the BACP membership and what that actually looks like, in reality, when we truly consider employment of the BACP qualified and fully trained members.

I think this has to be a fair criticism, that the BACP, as a membership body are not standing up for very many of their members (but only the elite Accredited members). I am talking about their many great 'registered' therapists, those whom have passed the computerised therapy proficiency examination, which means those who are then registered with the BACP today, good people that have already been *fully trained* and have a good level of competency, that are offering therapy to many people and caring well for them independently.

I am also glad to report that the witch-hunts, mainly in the past, are certainly not publicised and given to naming and shaming in the BACP magazine anymore.

However, since joining the BACP, I noticed that there is a BACP created hierarchy that is evidenced in many professions, this brings in further levels of *alleged* 'academic and therapeutic skills competence expertise and levels of care', with their stages of accreditation hoops we are supposed to jump through.

The first stage is to become a simple member, then the main hoop, is to pass their proficiency examination to become officially registered as qualified and on the BACP register. This we were told, is to show a therapist's academic competence, at the established standard of qualification level, by way of a 'registration' as the 'examined competence' first stage of the BACP ladder, where one is brought on to the accredited register. This is where one is to be listed as 'competent enough to advertise'

[Adds: and therefore surely competent enough, to be worthy to work, or otherwise why does the BACP allow them to be advertised as such on their registered listing.]

Incidentally, I heard from a lady member of the BACP, the other day, who had previously completed and passed her proficiency examination with the BACP, but informed me of her disgust, at suddenly finding out from a friend that her name and details were not on the accredited register – she searched and could not find her name anywhere, and when questioning the BACP admin, was coldly told,

"You let the BACP know that you were not seeing clients full time for a while, as you were taking, a well-deserved break, so we have removed you from the accredited register." But they had not told her she would be removed in that event, otherwise she would have explained that she was still working part -time.

So this poor lady, who is coming up to retirement age, had not even been told she was going to be removed. And to make matters worse, when she requested that she be put back on immediately, because at no time had she said she wanted to stop altogether and come off the register, she was then told bluntly by the admin, that they are

"not prepared to put her back on the register again, without her

paying for and undertaking the proficiency examination again."

But when she said she was furious (having spent good time and money to drive miles to sit the BACP exam, approximately only 18 months previously) and would go public and make a proper complaint of the matter, suddenly she was reinstated immediately. Customer satisfaction survey, anyone? You couldn't make it up!

Then we come to the next hoop, which is to then pay more and spend more time to get further 'Accreditation' (but wasn't that a 'register of training skills, as an accreditation' that members had done already?) and then pay more and spend more time to go up the ladder again to become a 'Senior Accreditation' (Why? To get the golden key to the special loo?) It all seems like a competition, to see who can get further up the ladder of academia and to be seen as a better therapist. Is it important for the BACP members to continue a status quest, to satisfy insecurities, of – 'Am I good enough yet?') and all the time sitting in a glass house of morals, teaching on dilemmas, integrity and ethics.

In my opinion, the BACP needs to look again at their process in membership accreditation structure, in what appears to be this academic BACP sausage factory, causing their often *fully trained and therefore very qualified and usually very caring members*, (sometimes having completed 5-8 years or more, of classroom attended, very in-depth psychotherapy training) into jumping through these unreasonable hoops, within this hierarchical system. One is tempted to ask, 'Is this simply an effort to bring in more money for the BACP, within the accreditation system?' Though, in the meantime, these poorly treated *'registered but not fully Accredited'*, members find it difficult to get regular paid work, why? because they do not fulfil the accreditation criteria, being laid down by the BACP itself, rolled out for the NHS and other employers, to pick it up and run with it, to hit our members where it really hurts, in the pocket, and worse, it also suggests that these great members are not good enough. They are being rejected by employers, on the grounds that the BACP are suggesting, for members who have not yet jumped through the higher hoops as they are not yet Accredited by what the employers are led to believe, that the BACP is the regulating body. And the latter, is totally Untrue!

This is ludicrous, because these members are '**already qualified**' and many are running private practices, or may have gained some low paid part time work, or they are having to do more volunteer work, to continue to qualify on the BACP Register, by getting supervised client hours in.

The real ethical hypocrisy going on, is around the real issue, adding salt to the wound, that many all have been led to believe, due to the rules and regulation proclaimed by the BACP, *et all*, and the threat of regulation within the profession, that the BACP have naturally become the regulatory body for Counselling. I also recall being told, a few years ago, that counsellors would all have to tape every client session soon, because the authorities would only allow us to continue in practice, if we complied with that order!).

But in the meantime, with regulation looming on the professional horizon of change, as a threat to all therapists, this meant that the somehow, the BACP seemed to slip suddenly into the position of counselling profession regulators!?

So primarily from that point onwards, we had begun to see the nailing down of the lids of the employment hierarchy on the grounds that BACP must be right. Then the NHS and general employers, occupational health schemes, insurance companies and solicitors, etc, all began to believe wrongly, that the BACP is a *regulating body* and not just a *membership organisation,* which is all the BACP currently exist as *(so how ethical is that?) it is in effect, a sin of 'omission' which comes across as a total hypocrisy, from those who are shouting morals and ethics to the rest of us.*

This is the rub, as the reason the NHS and other employers, are believing the BACP about standards and judgements on their own members competences, is because the BACP are allowing these employers to continue to believe that the BACP are our regulating body. *Which they clearly are not!*

It may well be that the BACP want to be a regulatory body, but they are not one, at the moment. So by making the NHS and employers believe that only 'Accredited' members, are the only ones who should be given jobs it continues to degrade its members and show a lack of care for those who they are supposed to be representing.

That is disgusting really and how is that helping their members. Many are great therapists and continue to study by researching and continuing professional development, but do not wish to become accredited, **when they have been sufficiently trained to start with** as advanced counsellors or psychotherapists. It is literally outrageous! No! You really couldn't make it up! Well could you?

There are many of us who say enough is enough and decide not to jump through the hoops of accreditation with the BACP now and quite a few are jumping ship unless this is rectified big time. Many others and myself, have personally sought Accreditation elsewhere, in quiet protest.

The BACP are insisting that their assessment and accreditation system is valid and obviously the various employers do not know the difference and continue to think the BACP are the ethical regulatory body, that therefore should know best and what the BACP message to the employers is saying, is that don't employ non- Accredited therapists. So now, the BACP are giving a strong message, which is morally wrong, **saying, their members need to be Accredited and not only 'trained', 'examined to be competent' and 'registered' as a 'fully paid-up' and 'qualified' as psychotherapists or counsellors**,

Now, it seems to be incorrectly believed by many, that the only employable and worthy members, are the elite, the Accredited ones. Does anyone else think this is wrong? Surely, they cannot continue this wrongdoing to their members?

I think it could be dangerous for the BACP and may possibly be considered, as a monopolies commission issue, or may even attract discrimination action, by its members, who have been fully trained and yet rejected badly, by its own representative body.

It really means, therapists need to pay lots of money, just to jump through further and more expensive hoops, *even after being fully trained* (which is very expensive) and which then stops these great trained therapists, being able to take good paying therapy jobs, because the BACP have now created an unethical inner and outer (by default – as I said, a sin of omission) by their unfortunate ladder system of entitlement, through further grades (more money again) **when the main training is fully sufficient, according to their proficiency exam, or why have the exam at all?**

It is not a good situation really. Surely the BACP needs to look to their laurels by recognising this blatant error and start to act ethically in this situation, instead of deflecting off to other issues and staying loyal to what appears to be, a *wrong system of status, for representations for their member's opportunities to work in the profession,* by perpetuating the myth.

One lives in hope, that those who pull the strings (usually the accredited, enlightened ones?) may eventually listen to the caring professionals they represent, without getting all defensive and reactive.

CHAPTER 23:
TRAINING METHODS

Primarily in private practice, with patients, as a psychotraumatologist and with many interactions directly and indirectly with other caring professionals, I have discovered many beautiful things as a spiritual person who became a psychotherapist and firmly believe that I am a wounded healer that enjoys the satisfaction of helping others on their journey into discovery, with the freedom to feel and liberation to be, yet my eyes have been opened to many difficult issues we face as independent professionals.

For a start there is the problem we face with the training levels that differentiate psychotherapists from counsellors, yet is not acknowledged widely enough right now. And in my opinion wrongly herds us all into the same level of competence within our profession, which is ludicrous.

Unfortunately the local colleges that were previously funded to teach counselling did not recognise psychotherapy as mainline enough to teach and deserve funding because it was usually post graduate training. What did they do?

Well the next thing that happened is that colleges managed to bring psychotherapy training into postgraduate levels by calling it counselling and gained the needed funding. From a business standpoint (all organisation require cash flow to survive) so I can understand the need to make something viable to the student body and the authorities governing the education system, but unfortunately we need to be real and recognise that it is a mistake to think that a basic counsellor qualified at a mere level-four diploma, is able to work at the same level as a psychotherapist, to put it blunt this is quite frankly, ridiculous.

Unfortunately, that is the message being put out there by the further education and higher education which has then been picked up by the media to no good end.

In not differentiating between the two different professions it means that many counsellors also enjoy their pseudo-clinical status and similarly they are unaware of the difference either.

We have noticed that even many advanced counsellors really have no idea what the difference actually is; therefore the media and often counsellors do not realise the vast scope and levels at which the psychotherapist has experientially trained to know and see from the language and behaviours of others; including what depth of repair the psychotherapist is able to accomplish, with even quite disturbed and damaged people.

When we add Trauma training to that psychotherapy understanding and continued personal study and research, there is a lot we may offer to Trauma patient's by way of this deeper experiential training and not just the simple talking cure.

Those of us who are informed also recognise that psychologists have not been required in UK to have personal psychotherapy which is quite criminal and a ridiculous scenario in these current days of information research and deeply informed evidence based standards of work, although some psychologists are encouraged to have counselling and must have 'clinical supervision' in their work (which is not therapy) and unfortunately, is usually performed by other senior psychiatrists or psychologists (who also have had no personal therapy to deal with their early life issues). This means that it really is "the blind, leading the blind" and we know instinctively what may happen to both of them.

Neither supervisor or supervisee are likely to be called to account for their unconscious acting out behaviours, because they are not aware of them at all, they are unconscious, whereas in psychotherapy training there is a lot of work done with the shadow and when faced with transference work and mirroring, we are able to integrate and contain, as we accommodate and work with this transference, and offer counter transference form the good parent position and the patient then may learn new life skills.

Because this psychology training has little experiential work at grass roots level, of care for a person, born out of personal experiences; it is obvious there is a lack of compassion and empathy where the doctor / patient relationship is concerned because the clinician has not had to deal with their own stuff prior to the work they are doing with their patients.

As professional psychotherapists in training issues often surface as students engage with their tutor's training material, often delivered in a lecture, or small group discussion, workshops, or as student one-to-one peer counselling / psychotherapy.

The students are then told by the tutors, regarding what we learn on the course and primarily anything we find unsettling or upsetting in any way or where the material causes discomfort in any way, to discuss the issues arising in their personal therapy, with the medical training model in mental health psychology that does not happen yet, even though in my opinion, it really should be the standard like it is for psychotherapists.

Whereas, this clinical psychology training, tends to promote an ethereal tick box, clinical mentality, which is totally different from the training, that a psychotherapist must have.

In psychotherapy training therapy usually goes much deeper into a person's issues and tends to bring out the trainee psychotherapists or patient's potential, and to explore and deal with personal problem behaviours such as passive aggression, uncontrollable explosive anger, envy jealousy, greed and extreme avoidance due to self-worth issues and fear or basic attachment issues to name but a few areas of concerns in hospitals and the NHS generally today.

There are many scenarios played out in the classroom using gestalt work in psychodrama and transactional analysis and other fitting therapies utilised as ways to find resolutions to the games we all play in defending ourselves or getting the attention we need and finding resolutions and often life changing revelation and breakthroughs.

The unconscious is explored together in personal therapy when the classroom gets too invasive and we need more help to deal with hurts or wounds and to understand ourselves and the hidden true self within the shadow of the false self.

Although we find this experiential training often brings resolve to many issues right there in class perhaps with group or the supervised peer therapy that takes place right there in the classroom sometimes, or when a student personally finds that 'Aha' moment all for themselves, which is discovered as we learn together and uncover many areas of early wounding.

We really do need to have psychotherapy and not just counselling, because psychotherapy has much more depth in training and we have more tools in our bag for would be counsellors and psychotherapists to learn and develop skills and insight as we are trained to a deeper experiential level of knowledge; and that enables us to challenge patients and make more accurate in depth interventions, yet from the same sensitive but engaging and caring position.

Therefore, students need to realise that our work is not just gaining head knowledge alone and to be great in all the theories as we need to be able to apply what we learn and not just make mental notes in our head or be able to understand enough to simply tick boxes but instead to experience the psychotherapy first hand to know what it feels like to be helped into a disintegration and helped to find yourself and put yourself back together with a psychotherapist facilitating and empowering us through those so important changes where we may learn to truly live healthier and happier lives.

Where necessary we are to make appropriate interventions and this involves transference and counter-transference as something to be welcomed for the client where they may realise new positive life experiences, for example, with the therapist perhaps in the re-parenting role and where the unconscious id drives are considered.

It could be that we recognise the Oedipus complex and need to discover and even offer other re-parenting reactions and for the patient's to learn new skills, where we act out a situation in the therapy room and truly become the 'good parent' so that the patient learns what it is like to have a good parent instead of the natural one that was not helpful or even neglectful and even critically abusive and so they eventually learn to self-nurture; with the therapist playing the role of the good parent and new positive input is offered.

The client will learn new ways of being in that scenario, all of which helps where a person was perhaps intimidated or dismissed and ignored and perhaps had no voice, rather than loved and encouraged, that becomes 'grist for the mill' and therefore welcomed as a new experiences for the patient in therapy, rather than to be cautioned by some police styled trainers, or supervisors, in some neurotic counselling organisations about that horrid 'counter transference', where we are warned about not reacting and transferring our issues and pain back onto the patients, often delivered to student counsellors. No surprise that this may be taught in some places, if the students are not expected to have psychotherapy and deal with their own issues, it could contribute to fear around the problems that type of client transference may bring up.

Then there is also the 'mirroring' in the dance of the therapeutic alliance, to a greater extent does not

There are many extremes and controlling elements within the caring professions and with patients in general.

It is my view there is also a real presence of professional jealousy and growing incompetence and lack of care that is damaging patients and therapists alike.

We need checks and balances within professional ethics and at the same time, to reach for transcendent ways to truly care for each other and recognise people as persons and not just as 'our work'. We are still facing a difficult time in this blame culture and the demand for evidence based results should be fair and not manipulated to balance the books or to just manage the numbers and let care go out of the window.

Finances have to be juggled and managers are needed but not in this top heavy management world of NHS health care. It should contain attitudes towards patients and professionals without prejudices and dump a lot of the political correctness, in this extreme faddish blame culture today (surely the latest madness within society).

Let me say right at the start; I have become very aware of my own vulnerabilities within this type of therapy work.

How easy it is to become the victim of wounded and angry fearful people (thinking of the counsellors drama triangle or the trauma quadrangle), especially those unfortunate people, we might call in the profession, 'vulnerable adults'.

Particularly in recognising how easy it is, as we train further to become an 'empath', to become burnt out by vicarious trauma, or by taking on some patient's problems that may be built up over a protracted time scale.

Who cares for the carers? Well we have to do that for ourselves, right? Please do take care of yourself, if you are party to so much pain and suffering. You may easily even get traumatised yourself! We will cover this later and explain the way we may take more care.

In the Convergence College of Psychotherapy we have developed a great system of psychotherapy. This is essentially Integrative and Transpersonal as we consider the whole person in this latest holistic psychotherapy teaching stream.

Our training in Convergence is very experiential and focuses on the uniqueness of the soul personhood and essence of the individual patient. We are concerned more with our 'relating with' rather than objectifying patients, unlike the NHS who offer an abstract clinical treatment plan, or make 'copy and paste' style assessments, with convenient psychiatric labels which are now hotly debated as not even evidence based. We therefore prefer to strip away the labels and get to know who the individual is and how best to treat the person.

Convergence College of Psychotherapy are now offering professional training, by teaching specialist treatments to individuals, who will become legitimate, licensed, fully skilled and qualified professionals as **Certified Trauma Clinicians.**

This training was primarily for their own diploma graduates, but more recently have opened the training to others externally, namely, to those professionals who may be qualified counsellors at Level-4, and to 'advanced' counsellor, or 'psychotherapeutic' counsellor (Level-5 diploma equivalent) or for fully qualified Psychotherapists (around Level-6/7). We may also extend this **Certified Trauma Clinician Training** to other professionals in the very near future in an effort to help sufferers access this important relief.

At Convergence College of Psychotherapy we offer full training from initial counsellor skills levels, up to fully qualified psychotherapists, in the five fold schema of modern psychotherapy, it's a © '*NeuroSomaSocioPsychoSpiritual*' *System,* developed to offer something quite different, in offering our body of Convergence counselling and psychotherapy students a much needed opportunity for a professional graduate specialism.

We do this by helping them to stretch a little further than even the professional masters levels in psychotherapy, and to go further than the BACP registered status, or even accredited status, and to train to qualify as a 'Psychotraumatologist' and Accredited member of the CPFI, with opportunities also to become accredited in Europe and the rest of the world as a Major Trauma specialist, fully equipped to remove and treat the most extreme of Major Trauma. Dealing with long term stress, PTSD, or protracted Trauma / C-PTSD and for some, possibly being trained to deal with an often accompanying Dissociation Identity Disorder (DID).

CHAPTER 24:
VICARIOUS TRAUMA

Carers think wrongly at times, that they are some sort of super-hero, like Superman or Superwoman and think because they are doing such a great job that they are invincible, but not so.

I have to confess here that because I became quite skilled in working with chaotic clients and ensuing trauma work and therefore I have been resolving so many Post Traumatic Stress Disorder problems and their related issues in so many broken lives, I neglected to take care of myself. That was ok until I began to start to unravel at times and became quite irritable and stressed myself and the obvious thought was these things are stressing me out and perhaps I am getting older and not being able to cope with the stresses so well as I sued to be able to do. Duh! Then I suddenly realised, whilst researching as usual, that I also had to accept that some of these traumas maybe due to the fact that I was suffering something called vicarious trauma.

You see, I was probably like so many others who are doing this work and have great empathy for the patients that I overlooked my own stress levels. How can that be, you might say? Well I was taking care of others and according to the many genuine testimonials from patients who thanked me for giving them their life back, it was quite easy to think I was fireproof, like others in the profession, because I could do the work well and felt great for a long time and I was very satisfied at the great variety of trauma issues that I could work with, students often uses to worry that they may not be able to leave the work at the office and yet I knew that the vast majority of professionals could do this very easily so I always encouraged fearful students to think positively in this real issue for every counselling professional.

But then there was this thing called burn-out that we heard about too. So my answer was glibly, "you will find ways to leave it at you're your office and this is part of the training; to learn how to detach from the work and the suffering and pain that comes with it. Empathy is surely our greatest gift to patients / clients and we know we could not offer congruent personal therapy without it?

Then the vicarious trauma hit me like a monkey on my back and some days my aggravation was quite intense and without my conscious recognition. Fortunately, when I read about the research into vicarious trauma it made perfect sense; though with some work with bilateral sound and some R & R (rest and relaxation - time out) helped me to come to terms with my vulnerability and then to find a position of acceptance helped a great deal to answer why I was getting upset and suffering stress myself. I realised at last I am surprisingly not invincible as the effects of vicarious trauma came to roost in my own personal tree.

It is just like the Post Traumatic Stress Disordered patients (PTSD). We help patients with the Trauma we find, and our empathy works to discharge the patient's trauma energy. It has come to light in neuroscience research that apparently the Amygdala, which is that part of the brain that shock is trapped in, and the Hippocampus is the part that has the calming effect to bring the hyper-arousal state down again.

This Calm state of the hippocampus is strangely communicated to one another as (m)other and baby are mirroring and (m)other is calming the baby with the hippocampus, my theory is that we too, as therapists, are strangely communicating to patients / clients by this phenomena all over the country and we may be woven together with others in the same way; just as they have found in equine or canine therapy (with horses or dogs).

At the same time, my personal theory which would need to be established correctly by some MRI style researching, I have no doubt that the individual therapist's Amygdala and a struggling therapist's hippocampus not calming the therapist would be susceptible to vicarious trauma by the steady stream of extreme suffering and anxieties brought on by the major Trauma our patients have suffered which is processing through our hippocampus in the therapy room, which may begin to also have an adverse effect on therapist.

If we are seeing the effects and sometimes hearing intimate details of many extreme traumas (even after the trauma has been dealt with, when the patients can talk about it easier) and the suffering causes exhaustion or similar stress, with work pressures that this type of patient will inevitably bring to bear, or if we are struggling with any stress by being over stretched in our own lives in any way ourselves. Just think about it for a moment, it makes sense to evaluate ourselves in light of this consideration and new information about vicarious trauma.

Surely, if your own hippocampus, working as a therapist and struggling with your own life issues, while dealing with traumatised patients, then you may surely begin to suffer from vicarious trauma yourself, through this medium. This is what I believe happened to me and it wasn't until I heard of vicarious trauma myself that I put two and two together and then became aware of vicarious trauma affect.

My symptoms showed up in these obvious ways now, but at the time the symptoms appeared surreal and were in some way strange reactions at the time it started to be noticed and at first I thought I was just getting in touch with my animus and becoming more in touch with my emotions, which was explained away, because I had become a mature psychotherapist, methinks at the time, what else could it be?

So for example vicarious trauma hit home to me when I could

not understand why I would begin to become quite emotional at the drop of a hat. I am not talking about crying at Lassie, but I had begun to find emotional when seeing things in the newspapers regarding personal hurts in acts of violence and suffering which seemed to suddenly bring me easily into the arena of traumatised feelings myself, where I would go further than empathy and really feel very impacted internally and feel the pain and had to turn away from the thoughts that the sufferer may well be experiencing and would be feeling quite sad and low and feeling pained, in some events I read about, my imagination would go wild and empathy went off the scale to the point of real pain and distress as I tried to repress the feelings and distract myself.

I also found I was easily irritated and thought it must be just a little hypertension going on, I also would stress to the point of going red in the face when I got upset, so with a loving advice from my doctor wife I began to check my blood pressure and made an appointment to see the doctor to find out if something was wrong with me physically. Having various tests and as a non-smoker and non-drinker and having little wrong with me my GP not only confirmed I was ok but told me at my age I was her case study and whatever I was doing to keep doing it, so I was lulled into a false sense of security really and dismissed the other symptoms of stress as just down to my age and having to work with difficult chaotic patients and certain types of demanding students at times; as this was just my caring self, by trying to calm and make sense of the work and the world at any one time.

I thought, maybe I just need a bit more exercise, as diet (nutrition is my wife's thing and she helps me so much to eat well) and exercise was taken care of, yet the symptoms ensued.

This covert effect of trauma has a tendency to creep up on you just like this happened in my subjective experience it happens often when you are not aware of it. When you are feeling strong it works its way in and develops like a cancer in your emotional brain.

Vicarious Trauma can also develop into a full blown PTSD and can affect you in the same way, as it is sometimes just like the last straw that breaks the Camel's back, so to speak.

I came to a point where I realised that my own quite strong empathy for others actually got the better of me. So although we can do this work without seemingly being affected by the emotional stress induced while working, don't think you are fire proof as it might just bite you in the rear when you are blindsided by even your own capability to initially detach as a therapist

However, once I began to realise what was happening to me I immediately started to use bilateral sound therapy and bio-feedback control as I recognised the stresses were taking their toll and began to take more time off to relax and do the things I wanted to do.

CHAPTER 25: CO-DEPENDENCY

Due to the co-dependent element, whom are regularly drawn into this caring profession, we rarely recognise our weaknesses and vulnerabilities, because we get so used to putting other people's feelings and issues as our priority of care every day; so it is so easy to be unaware of things creeping up on us, over time, or things building up, inside of our psyche, without our notice.

Therefore, this is a very important chapter for carers to learn more or be reminded to simply be more vigilant, regarding themselves and their feelings, when out of the therapy chair, as well as while they are in it.

Yes any self-respecting therapist is well aware of usually parking the patient's stuff that sticks to us when we leave the office and we try to release and pour our emotional baggage back into the filing cabinet before we leave for home but it doesn't always work even for the most qualified, competent and experienced of therapists.

We need to establish some sort of warning system. It is important not only to have a supervisor who knows you well, but more important to have at least one or two others, particularly if you have no spouse or partner, who also knows you well and to watch for signs of burn out or irritability or sensing that you are exhausted or defensive or confused or forgetful. These are all signs of a therapist metaphorically picking up more stuff than they can chew.

Therapists need to get help from their support network in raising a flag of concern if things start to take a down turn. Taking care of ourselves by being observant of any change in our mood swings is essential so mindfulness of our third eye outside of therapy and a network of supportive carers and close family supporters should negate these episodes and keep us cool.

If you are a therapist try to write some notes, to remind you, of the important points you need to remember about trauma and your own personal discoveries around the concept of Trauma and your therapy experience, at the back of this book. It may surprise you what comes up. And do try to keep a sense of humour when you are working, and remember to smile and laugh as much as you are able, because that is healing too.

Check yourself with the various lists at the back of this book.

CHAPTER 26: PRO-BONO WORK

We made a policy decision at Convergence to attempt to treat everyone who comes to us for help. That is regardless of their issues or their financial position, so we endeavour to overcome any financial hurdle stopping us from offering therapy to those who are in real need, and we often do pro-bono work in this difficult area of Trauma.

We suggest our mature students and graduates do the same in all mental health work and we believe that it is important to offer at least 10% of our prospective patients/clients who may be poorer, to access our pro-bono work. This is while they may be working as a 'student' therapist, and when they eventually become 'qualified' and hopefully where they work in their personal private practice, or even if they are employed by anyone else, to at least try to attempt to influence that same organisation in some way, to put something back into our humane effort of truly caring, by offering this professional 'pro-bono' work to the poor, wherever we are able.

Many reasons may be stopping people from getting the help they need when they need it but at least we can offer something, as caring individuals, to ease their suffering.

Whenever I see a documentary around those suffering Complex PTSD, like wounded or simply pensioned off ex-forces members of recent war zones that are still suffering PTSD and where they are not accessing real and lasting '*Trauma Relief*', and explain their daily fight to contain feelings and remain sane it upsets me so much to think we have therapists ready to help who have been trained in modern Trauma therapy, at a cost today for sure, but surely it's a worthwhile investment.

I offered at the time to give free therapy to any local people affected by any of the disasters who had to deal with victims or was involved in recent years, of the Manchester Bombings and Grenfell Tower to call on us and we would help them but strangely we had not even one call even though we are in the Midlands and yet we know that these sufferers will come out of the woodwork eventually when the shadow gets the better of them or someone, in due time, points them in the right direction to get help.

Obviously I do recognise that many victims did get help and do get help at crisis times now from volunteer Trauma specialists nearer to them and that is great, but the fallout is also enormous especially in vicarious Trauma within families or friendships and simple onlookers too. One just wonders what training the so called trauma care specialists have actually had, knowing the systems in place in the NHS at the moment in the UK.

Who will find the time to listen to these poor unfortunate people and refer them to Major Trauma Relief Therapy Specialists and not simple counsellors or psychologists with inadequate training, that have tried to deal with these problems and may have left so much undone in terms of stopping the suffering long term. If I was a fly on the wall at times…

Let's all try to educate the general public and begin to help those still suffering Trauma effects in society. They need to know they no longer need to suffer in silence today when there is better Trauma Therapy facilities on offer.

Are you still suffering Trauma symptoms?

STOP thinking you have to accept this, It is a lie, It's simply untrue, as we have new ways to help. It is Fake News!

Find real help, contact us and we will endeavour to help you find someone locally, because you no longer need to have those symptoms if you have been treated correctly.

Please understand that all Major Trauma symptoms can be alleviated and removed forever with George Booty's

© *Virtual Brain Re-Set* ™ *Therapy*.

CHAPTER 27: ONLINE HELP

For those in foreign countries or difficulties over transportation problems and are perhaps desperate to get help, until we see more trained clinicians working in other countries, we are prepared and able to work with many Trauma issues, even over a video call by the internet, particularly where finances and distance is a real issue.

Obviously with this kind of work, we would want to teach and other mental health practitioner, or at least a medic/senior nurse carer on hand, to aid the patient, in case internet problems occur. It is important we all help safeguard the suffering patient online.

Even language problems have been overcome online, in advance, by the use of a simple interpreter for dire emergency cases. We have worked like this in the past to great effect.

I am hoping to bring more focus on these issues by speaking out, unfortunately this may trouble those in authority, yet it needs to be highlighted and is merely my attempt to get more attention to bear on the fact that we have psychotherapies now that have moved on in understanding and levels that our professional forbears could only have dreamt of being able to understand and to be able to offer our newer techniques to deal with all this Trauma suffering in the world.

We offer specialist and 'Certified Trauma Training'

Please help me release the sufferers by helping them to find appropriate Psychological Trauma Therapy with trained experienced psychotherapists whom have also trained as specialist clinicians and some as psycho-traumatologists instead of simple low level basic counsellors at Diploma level-4, perhaps with a simple trauma informed certification, or even as Advanced level-5 Counsellors, registered, or even accredited BACP counsellors who still lack the necessary skills and expertise in training.

These counselling skills levels above do not ensure truly effective work in this 'specialist' area and it is important to establish the need for real 'psychotherapists whom have trained as real Trauma Clinicians' to be able to work in this specialised field and offer truly effective methods. So it is important to train certified professionals, who may work safely with patients and to treat their patients as individuals and persons, not just making use of unrealistic treatments, to move them on the ineffective conveyor belt of corruption that is currently going on as this operation is literally a terrible treatment plan for Trauma sufferers.

It has to be said too that many counsellors are great at what they do, but with minimal diploma training, especially with a lack of training in higher levels of psychotherapy, even though they may have attended many non-effective bolt-on style treatments and so many cpd seminars and short courses are offering outdated methods, and nobody seems to know, or even care. So much for the alleged *trauma informed* counselling that goes on today.

Severe Mental Health problems require a complete training in psychotherapy, as the solid basis enabling clinicians to truly engage with a patient safely within their larger scope and understanding which then leads on to further training in Psycho-Trauma at a deep level; so that these clinicians may deal effectively once and for all time with all the terrible PTSD affect symptoms, and at the same time the fall out could have caused other issues, which may include substance misuse, psychosis, personality disorders and particularly the life changing prevailing effect in the sufferer's family and their damaged relational conditions.

What we may offer here at Convergence today is truly amazing. I am so happy to help my patients find a peace and calm that they could not find prior to the therapy we offer them and that is simply a complete healing with no more nightmares, flashbacks, startle responses, avoidance issues, or further symptoms that sufferers experience with PTSD or Complex PTSD. We also tend to get depression sufferers out of depression within two to twelve weeks, on average.

We do know that research is currently being carried out in relation to the way a sufferer's philosophy of life and relationship may change after Trauma therapy which is not exclusive to our Convergence therapies, but is something that has been reported from all effective trauma therapies around the globe and we continue to work in this area too.

What is most irksome in my work, is the nonsensical suffering going on. When I think about all the many TV programs in the media, and documentaries where journalists are interviewing sufferers and the members of our own forces in particular, having had ineffective therapies (by comparison with ours) where they are supposed to **Help our Heroes** – And I hear the repeated mantra of "I have been told I just have to learn to live with this trauma, so I guess I will have to soldier on". It's a lie, a Myth! This is simply not so, its all about money, the therapy is here, but sadly the NHS or any local authority do not want to pay for it. It is specialised treatment so they just offer disgraceful silly alternatives to appease the rank and file.

Help is at hand. Yes it really is! so why can't we give the help?

Our heroes returning from war zones and also civilian victims of the recent ISAL, or other terror group bomb attack victims, or victims of natural disasters and the terrible accidents from buried land mines, or unexploded bombs and the incredible impact of war zones on the vulnerable families, whom have suffered PTSD and even stricken journalists suffering as a result of their work and the sights they witness, or crash investigators and accident victims across the board, surely we could do more to bring this modern aid in Trauma treatment to their attention?

These poor people are all Trauma victims and so many have continued to suffer for decades, long after the Traumas were initially experienced, due to a lack of affective facilities offered them. It saddens me so much to see all that unnecessary pain caused to the sufferers and their respective families, which have also suffered the fall-out from this epidemic of suffering.

It also upsets me to hear these PTSD sufferers have had to live with the pain and dis-ease thinking that is normal and anyone who has Trauma should accept their suffering as 'par for the course' so to speak and they should expect to continue suffering. Why has nobody in the mental health authorities told them that help really is available and within reach for the asking.

For the most part I believe it is ignorance, as I am sure for honest carers, it can only be for lack of information and in many cases could also be due to all the nonsensical administrations today, where decision makers in the Mental health services have tried to sweep this matter under the financial carpet.

Obviously it costs money to employ professionally trained specialist clinicians to deal with this important and specialised therapy, which is a current tragedy that will no doubt haunt these authorities in the future and their consciences will be pricked regarding their lack of concern, so who knows? The system might change eventually, if enough of us advertise what is going on at last.

We all know in many cases it is simply the greedy bean counters (big money corporates) that make the directives. The percentages need to stack up in these financial organisations where in some cases the powers to be make decisions to ignore the needs of the people.

Corporations seek to get their 'bang for buck' investments, so they are driven towards non-acceptance, of the real fact, there is a higher need for this truly specialised treatment (costing money) buy it really must be paid for, rather than these lies to placate the victims and their families, which is destroying the lives of many families as I write, in fobbing-off the poor suffering Trauma victims, with poorly-effective treatments offered through the NHS.

Truth is, that Trauma Victims are being sent to counsellors using methods that attempt to limit the symptoms, but do not resolve the shock and therefore get rid of the symptoms, an outcome that is truly contemptable.

Many counsellors are still using outdated methods that are only based in long term 'time healed' methods, or some professionals are simply told that they are unable to work with sufferers to alleviate PTSD because there needs to be at least one month before we may call the condition PTSD, so we are not expected to treat the patient with PTSD ethically, due to the rules of the psychiatric manual (currently DSM-V), it seems.

But what about our underlying duty of care and our moral focus here? To give Trauma Therapy for PTSD according to the psychiatric diagnostic manual - 'until they are 'time qualified to present with full blown PTSD' or using debriefing style trauma focused CBT (tfCBT) which is still only cognitive, mindful based counselling, at best.

There are also other ineffective ways being offered for these extreme trapped shock Trauma situations too, such as the equine or canine therapy, which it has to be said, is extremely helpful in calming and bringing distraction to an anxious patient for sure and it brings a sense of real well-being, as research has suggested recently.

It works because the hippocampus of the animal helps calm the individual, but we need to ask, will this alternative kind of therapy get rid of the trapped Trauma shock in the same way as 'our © **Virtual Brain Re-Set**^{TM} therapy? We think not!

So please stick with these more robust and effective modern methods, to fully resolve Major Trauma.

It needs to be methods that get real resolution results, to evidence a return to healthy behaviour and sufferers being able to do things they could not really comfortably do before, and not just given simple coping mechanisms to ease some of the pain. We know our methods are truly the best there is and they work really well.

Many other so called interventions are based on price to deliver to patients and may be very ineffective compared to our treatments.

CHAPTER 28: - HANDOUT -

This is for Trauma clients going into therapy treatment
Find this on the web site too

HANDOUT – 1.

The Lifescript Clinic of Harley Street - Treatment Centre for Trauma & Psychotherapy

Trauma – Post Traumatic Stress Disorder PTSD or C-PTSD. Both Low & High Intensity Therapy (LIT/HIT) and CET / CBPT.

Trauma is often associated with combat stress, or child abuse and this is effective with all types of Trauma and for such things as major accidents, rape, violence and all kinds of extremely shocking events.

Client Readiness & Safety Protocols:

1). If trauma is related to: crime, a victim or a police officer and there has been a critical incident that will need a legal deposition, or a trial testimony, that maybe required, because under trauma therapy the image of the event may fade or blur or even disappear completely. Although a patient may be able to tell what has occurred they may not be able to offer a vivid or detailed account of the event.

2). Trauma disturbances in therapy: Patients should realise and hold onto the knowledge that an uncomfortable disturbance in session or between sessions, is when the trauma material is being 'released' and then be able to feel comfortable in experiencing a high level of vulnerability, or a lack of control and any physical sensations from the event/s that may well be part of the historical trauma. It means that the patient must be willing to tell the clinician the truth regarding what they are experiencing. Although patients do not need to disclose details of their trauma, it is imperative that they are willing to experience the emotions in front of their clinician and reveal whatever emotions emerge and to report accurately the nature and intensity of these emotions.

3). Feeling Raw between sessions: When the patient withholds they are more likely to experience higher abreaction–level material, in session or between sessions, without the appropriate clinical support. Therefore suicide ideation or suicide attempts are more likely when the patient withholds information from the clinician, about the intensity of emotions. Patient's need to know they should call on the clinician if difficulties are experienced between any trauma sessions and therefore may need to be prepared for additional urgent sessions to reduce disturbances. There is a need to maintain a strong therapeutic alliance with clinician due to the potential for additional between sessions disturbance.

4). Dissociative Disorders – Dissociative Identity Disorder (DID) also previously termed as a Multiple Personality Disorder, also Mutism, or other disorders occurring. Please ensure patient fills in the <u>Dissociation Questionaire form</u>, particularly if experiencing major disturbances, like combat stress.

5). Debriefing: It is important to have enough time to debrief a patient at the end of each session regarding the individual trauma and experiences, if not then the client could continue the processing between sessions at a higher level of disturbance. In extreme cases where client is experiencing major disturbances <u>there may be a need to take double sessions</u> while abreactions come into normalised processing and to readjust session bookings in light of this information.

6). Patient Log: Please keep a log of any memories, dreams, thoughts, and situations that are in any way disturbing. Keeping a journal helps the clinician to target obvious needs that should be treated. It will also point out to your clinician any dysfunctional patterns of behaviour that may need attention. Patients should realise it is important not to proceed too quickly and yet to understand that further disturbances are a natural part of trauma processing. And it is important for patients to "let whatever happens, happen" as it's all part of the healing process, so if there is disturbance, or if none, it's all part of the healing journey and a natural outworking.

7). Medications: If patient is already being stabilised by GP / Psychiatrist / CPN, on medications, such as benzodiazepines, or alternative SRI's, or anti-psychotics, etc. although the meds do not appear to completely block the trauma therapies, nevertheless, experience proves, some traumas need to be reprocessed again, after patient comes off the meds. Clinicians have also reported that if a patient is asked to re-access the treated memory after meds have been discontinued, trauma can return with approximately 50% of its original associated disturbance. Therefore a combat stress with a SUDS (Subjective Units of Disturbance) level of '10' after reducing to '0', but when the patient came off meds it could return back to a '5' on the SUDS scale, which is pretty high and may not discharge naturally. Therefore Patient's and particularly their GP's, really need to be educated that prescribing meds for 'Trauma' will often increase the overall time scale of psychological trauma treatment, so there is a need to look for the deeper signs before prescribing for high anxiety.

8). Patient support check: It is important that the patient has support (family or friends) to be around, to check on patient over the time of extreme trauma work being done, to monitor the SUD levels of disturbance with patient and continue to support and to particularly remind patient that the necessary reprocessing continues to release, or even reveal other trauma and therefore there may be some disturbing material brought to surface which should be released naturally, in-between therapy work sessions, however, be sure to inform about anything too harsh, while in session. Process usually discharges emotions through sleep, in the dream state. My saying is '*The Dreaming Brain keeps you sane*'. Good sleep therefore is imperative. Ensure you have our 'sleep tips' handout. The relevant clinician will deal with informed disturbance in the following sessions.

9). Trauma abreactions - Symptoms to be aware of:
Imagine a field suddenly being ploughed up. The emotions are being stirred up like this and much comes to the surface. Different affects such as physical tiredness, which comes suddenly as the body begins to relax, whereas previous to trauma therapy there was an emotional holding on (even aggressive or controlling behaviour). Now as there is a resurfacing and gradual resolution of trapped emotions, with therapy, other affects may manifest, we call this post traumatic reaction. Affects may be; Exhaustion, Irritability, Swings, or Lows, in Mood, Depression, Jumpy, Night (or sleep) Sweats, Shakiness, Low/High level Dissociation, Distracted, Intrusive thoughts, Anger, Denial, Tearful, Sad, Confused, Forgetful, Sleepy. And possibly Grief, Loss and often Guilt and Shame. All this is expected and yet some may experience very little disturbance initially, only pure relief.

10). Monitoring effects & Concluding Therapy:
Our patient/clinician contract states a need for you to give at least 4 week's notice, to end therapy treatment, or regular sessions, this covers our duty of patient care and the normal demands of our business flow, with patients/client work. There is a need to monitor the withdrawal of our support and to tie up any loose ends, or discharge any emotional issues, brought up, in or around, your therapy. We also have a duty of care to monitor the longer term effects of the trauma work, with follow up appointments, at intervals of 1 month, 3 months and specifically about one year after trauma work.

11). Safe Trauma Containment:
It is crucial for your safety, that you are able to cooperate, so you may properly relax in session, with the clinician's normal help, and it also helps if you are able to hear well (inform us of 'hearing' problems) and see reasonably clearly (inform us of any 'sight' issues). And be intellectually able to follow and fully submit to clinicians instructions (let us know if you don't understand).
It is very useful to practice your breathing, the 'Benson Technique', between sessions night and morning and to be able to sit still in therapy and be able to use your imagination, before we attempt therapy each session. We use mainly soft Low Intensity Therapy (LIT) and where necessary we also use High Intensity Therapy (HIT).

12). Children & Adolescents:
We will work with Children from 10-16 with children present and Adolescents between 16-18 with parental consent. But we need parents to stay with children (under 16) by watching at a safe distance (we will inform where to observe therapy). Children under this age would need to be assessed, along with at least one parent, before offering our commitment of any immediate help.

12). **Existing Patients only – The Emergency Contact Number:**
Ask for the number and write this down immediately.

.... In case of difficulties between sessions.
Call this number and Give your name and phone number (repeat in case it's a bad line) and explain briefly the problem and we will try to text you to make another appointment or call you back.

NOTE: We usually leave some space for emergency appointments on Fridays, so that you may have extra cover, if required, over the week-end. Otherwise you will need to attend A & E for urgent help.

CHAPTER 29:
TRAUMA AND SLEEP

We need to help our clients at times, because we often are looking at people who have become totally dysregulated in sleep and general lifestyle due to the alarming suffering they have gone through and the wrong habits they have created in their own lives. At times, this is learned helplessness behaviour from dysregulated, or chaotic parents, or the inconsistent input of one of the parents undermining the authority of the other parent, so nothing works well. My book '**Chaotic Client & Self**' in the '**Booty's Notes**' series, which offers guidance to work with this type of chaotic client.

I also need to explain briefly that this becomes a re-parenting of one's client that is not looking after themselves properly. For example, I have often needed to take my depression clients back to basics and show them about the need for REM sleep to dissipate anxieties and worries to get a good night's sleep. I usually do this by explaining about child rearing and what works and doesn't work with children. Why? Simply without being patronising, it is because some clients act like misguided children who have lost their way.

I will explain to client's in chaos, that we need to go back to these basics because something is not working properly in their lives right now, I further explain, when you have a small child there is a need to teach a child to be regulated, so in the evening to begin to get ready for bed, you will obviously turn off the TV, or the computer. We get the child to put their toys away. We would then have a time of calming (Dad does not need to wind them up with boisterous games, at this point) while they get undressed and then ushered into the bath. They are then dressed in their PJ's (night clothes) and perhaps have some supper, although health wise, the milk and 'cookies' maybe not for today. And then it's supervising that their teeth are brushed well and off we go up the wooden hill (stairs) and this gives a clear signal it's time for bed.

Once we arrive at the bedroom we go in and close the curtains, tuck them into bed and tell them a happy bedtime story. We kiss them goodnight and while saying "goodnight, see you in the morning", we leave the bedroom door ajar and leave the light on and walk back down the stairs to have 'me' time.

As we begin to settle down to relax, maybe five minutes later, we suddenly hear the sound of tiny feet trotting down the stairs and our child appears at the bottom, rubbing their eyes and saying, "I can't sleep!" So what do you do now?

I wait for the answer? Well. Some parents will pet them and play with them again, or just let them cuddle up on the chair, while the parent continues to watch an adult soap opera, or give the child another drink, or just let them play on the floor again and get all their toys out again. Or to rub it in here, I often joke and say we could put a film on the TV, like 'The Chainsaw Massacre', and scare them to half to death. Of course the clients get what I am trying to get them and begin to understand and then come the excuses. Like, I've tried to get more sleep but it doesn't work. I quickly follow up with the good parent once they realise the child is not sick, will immediately take the child straight back upstairs and put them back into bed again and say it's not morning and you have to go to sleep now it's night time and we all have to sleep at night. If the child comes down 50 times in a night what do you do? You take it back upstairs as you must win this one as a parent. You must regulate your child to get healthy sleep and look after their well-being. It is the same in other areas, such as drinking enough water, eating properly and exercising, all are important in self-regulation.

Handout-2

Tips for a good night's sleep follow:

- **Go to bed earlier:** You may not even think you will sleep. But if you normally go to bed very late and always wake up tired then you need to change your sleeping habits.
- **Avoid drinking too much:** having a little drink in the evening may seem as if it helps you, because you fall asleep quicker when you go to bed, but you are almost certain to wake up in the middle of the night, once the alcohol has been metabolised and your body is in withdrawal because that wakes you up, which is apart from the fact that mixers, like coca cola, etc, are dietics.
- **Don't exercise before bed:** Do something relaxing before bedtime. Avoid taking any exercise or exerting yourself within 2 hours of planning to go to sleep (sexual activities could be kept light) as strenuous exercise will be likely to keep you awake. Do exercise but try to do it much earlier in the day or evening, just the same as having a big meal, better to eat earlier for the same reasons.
- **Have a milky drink:** or perhaps some camomile tea before bedtime (not ordinary Tea and especially not Coffee, because of the high Caffeine intake).
- **Enjoy a relaxing warm bath:** or shower before going to bed.
- **Sleep on a comfortable mattress:** it might be that yours has become worn and has sagged, even without you realizing it. Check it out from the side view.
- **Block out as much light:** when you sleep, darken the bedroom as much as you can. Use thick curtains, or some blackout blinds can be a very effective way of preventing being woken up and blinded by the daylight.
- **Use the bedroom primary for sleep:** If you have spent a lot of time in bed because of injury, illness or pain, you may be more accustomed to using the bedroom as

a 'living room' like routinely watching television in it, or even for receiving visitors, especially of you are renting a room or lodging with a family or even back with good old Mum and Dad, so it could be that you are reading newspapers, magazines, or listening to music. Doing anything before sleep and that keeps your brain alert, is not going to be helpful. Soothing music may be good, but loud music with an insistent beat is definitely not a good idea. Scary movies are also out! Making love is good, because although sex stimulates, it discharges energy and so doesn't adversely affect sleep and can relax you to easily slip into sleep, but take it easy tiger!

- **Block out noise:** you may try wearing earplugs, especially if your partner snores, or if noise disturbs you from outside.

- **Make sure your bedroom temperature:** is set at the correct degree to sleep in at night. Ensure that you are not too hot or cold in bed. Ideal temperature is apparently 16-18 degrees. But take advice on this from your doctor.

- **Try spraying lavender:** you may scent the room, or perhaps use a lavender pillow. Many people find that the scent helps to induce sleep.

- **Stay awake all day:** Do not be tempted to nap at lunch time, or at any time when you might suddenly feel sleepy, even though you probably feel anxious to get any sleep you can. Power-naps are great for 'non-sufferers' not you.

- **Don't lie awake:** having anxious, or angry thoughts. Use one of the Convergence techniques we describe for inducing relaxation and then take yourself off in your imagination to your safe place, a peaceful, secure and safe, quiet place. Give yourself the suggestion every so often that *"sooner rather than later, I can drift off into a sound refreshing sleep and wake up feeling well and refreshed in the morning, at… (…such and such a time)"*.

- **If you wake up in the night:** never reward the brain for remaining awake. Some people decide, after lying awake for half an hour, to get up and watch a film, or go to have something to eat, or put the iPad on or check the phone. By that 'rewarding' this just encourages the brain to wake up every night, usually around the same time, so instead, if you are not sleeping within 30 minutes, get up and do an extremely 'boring' task that you really loathe doing. Like chores! It might be working your way through a pile of ironing; doing your accounts, waxing the floor; sewing on buttons; or filling cracks in the wall in preparation for decorating. (of course we realise some people enjoy such activities!). You could even invent a boring task, such as standing on one leg whilst reading the telephone directory quietly out loud!!! As soon as you are really tired, however, abandon the tasks and go back to bed.

- **Repeat the chores:** only if you are still awake 30 minutes later, or wake up again.

Remember my mantra:

The Dreaming Brain Keeps You Sane!

This is where we process all the worries and Traumas, while we may attend Trauma therapy, the time in between sessions is also part of the healing journey and you need to work at the healing part by sleeping right. If you are a sufferer, then you have to make an effort to do this, for your own personal well-being.

CHAPTER 30: - MY LISTS -

Worst Trauma experiences

Listed and scored 0 – 10. Ten being the highest energy felt.

MY TRAUMAS

Scaled (before therapy)

MY TRAUMAS

Scaled (after therapy)

MY PERSONAL TRAUMA NOTES

My philosophical view of Relationships and Love, both before and after therapy?

MY PERSONAL VICARIOUS TRAUMA CHECKS.

Let me say right at the start; I have become very aware of my own vulnerabilities within this type of therapy work.

How easy it is to become the victim of wounded and angry fearful people (thinking of the counsellors drama triangle or the trauma quadrangle), especially those unfortunate people, we might call in the profession, 'vulnerable adults'.

Particularly in recognising how easy it is, as we train further to become an 'empath', we may (regardless of the assurances of experienced counsellors or tutors) eventually become burnt out by vicarious trauma, or by taking on some patient's problems that may be built up over a protracted time scale.

Who cares for the carers? Well we have to do that for ourselves, right? Please do take care of yourself, if you are party to so much pain and suffering. You may easily even get traumatised yourself!

DO A QUICK INVENTORY

Be very honest with yourself. Senses are heightened – check using the 3rd Eye within therapy, and check the Observer-self outside of therapy; Feelings of Avoidance - with certain types of issues, or people; Feelings around Intrusion; Feelings of Hyper-Arousal - over-sensitivity; Feelings of threat – fight, flight or flop; Irritability and Aggravation levels; Any specific Trauma Triggers; Uncomfortable Sensations in the body; Stress levels increased – weight gain, larger midriff, comfort eating; Immune system diminished – colds and flu or worse symptoms; Check Psychosomatic illnesses – IBS, allergies, urinary track infections, other infections hanging around; Thyroid flare-ups; Skin complaints – also associated with internalised anger. Unable to relax and stay on the go; or when made to relax, hit with tiredness, feeling exhausted – or actual exhaustion and unable to stay awake and a desire to sleep longer; Try to research other signs of Trauma / burn out.

Begin now, by writing-up your own tell-tale signals here...

YOUR TELL-
TALE SIGNS

Continued ….

Published here by Kindle Direct Publishing through Amazon. Printed in Poland by Amazon, Fulfilment Poland, Sp.

For information address: Please write to Convergence College Publications—393 Acorn House Midsummer Boulevard, Milton Keynes. Buckinghamshire. England. U.K. MK9 3HP.

Our usual fees are established on the web site at:- www. talktherapy4u. org.

Email to: office at talktherapy4u. org .

Please do get in touch with us if you want to explore more in training, or would like us to give a talk to any support groups, or community services, or churches, or other caring organisations, who may wish to be enlightened in Trauma work.

Alternatively, for further training or personal accreditation, please contact the Convergence College of Psychotherapy co-ordinator office at convergencecollege. Org, or contact the CPFI directly for student or full membership or personal registration, or accreditation, at:- office at cpfi. co. uk.

Adds: It is my sincere hope that you enjoy the contents of this book and perhaps even write a note when you have the time and let us know about your own personal experiences, either as a clinician, or as a sufferer and particularly if this book has helped you in any way.

We are continually researching this material. Please feel free to write to the email addresses above for myself, **Dr George Booty** at **Convergence College of Psychotherapy** or to the accrediting research Institute, **'Central Professional Foundation & Institute' (CPFI)**. Please ensure you copy and paste to the second emails, simply to increase the chances we receive it, in this day of modern technology that is not fallible. If you would like a reply email, you may want to add our address to your email address book too, or we may all go down the spam path together (grins). We are eager to hear from you all.

CRISIS HELP

Annex - A

Useful further information and/or links.

Info on Current NICE General Guidelines on Trauma;

For Recommendations about Post-traumatic stress disorder and Guidance from 'NICE'

https://www.nice.org.uk/guidance/ng116/chapter/Recommendations

More LINKS:-

EFT - NICE

https:// www.nice. org. uk/sèarch?q=eft.

Also Trauma focused CBT

https://www.evidence.nhs.uk/search?q=trauma+focused+cbt

Other helps for Trauma and suicide:
If you or a loved one has experienced sexual assault, you're not alone and there is help available. To be connected with a trained staff member from a sexual assault service provider in your area for the - National Sexual Assault Telephone Hotline.

Also Lilli Hope Lucario's great web site is useful at;

www.healingfromcomplextraumaandptsd.com

Suicide Prevention Resources:-

999 and **112** is the national emergency number in the United

Kingdom **111**, Option **2**, is the National Health Services'
First Response Service for mental health crises and support.
This is not available in all areas of the country yet.

Samaritans: (http:// www.samaritans. org/)
is a registered **charity** aimed at providing
emotional support to anyone in distress or at risk
of **suicide** throughout the **United Kingdom**.
They provide a 24/7, free crisis line, as well as local branches.

Samaritans Helpline can be reached at **116 123**.

Samaritans' previous hotline number, 08457 90
90 90, is no longer in use. Calling this line may
result in charges for call forwarding

SHOUT Contact:
Shout: (https:// www.giveusashout. org/) is the UK's first free
24/7 text service for anyone in crisis anytime, anywhere.
It is a place to go for those struggling to cope
and in need of immediate help.
Shout exists in the US as 'Crisis Text Line' but this is the first
time the tried and tested technology has come to the UK.

Also there is the 'Get Help' Text – **85258.**

Campaign Against Living Miserably: (https://www. the calm zone.
net/) is a registered charity based in **England**. It was launched in March
2006 as a campaign aimed at bringing the **suicide** rate down among
men aged 15–35. It has a limited-hour phone and webchat options.

CALM (Nationwide) can be reached at 0800 58 58
58 (available every day from 5PM to midnight).

CALM (London) can be reached at 0808 802 58
58 (available every day from 5PM to midnight).

CALM webchat can be found at https://www.thecalmzone.net/
help/get-help/ (available every day from 5PM to midnight).

Victims First: If you are a victim of Abusive, or
Controlling behaviour. Call 0300 1234 148.

www. victims-first. org. uk.

Help for Heroes:- To Get Support call your nearest Recovery Centre

North: Phoenix House, Catterick 01748 834148

West: Plymouth Recovery Centre 01752 562179

East: Chavasse VC House, Colchester 01206 814880

South: Tedworth House, Tidworth 01980 844200

Also getsupport at helpforheroes. org. uk
There is also an Armed Forces Covenant being signed by
many organisations and authorities now: to ensure Ex-
forces are to be treated fairly. Check to see if your local
council has signed up to that and contact them.

For LGBT - Call the UK LGBT crisis intervention and suicide prevention hotline, or google **the Trevor project.** https://www. thetrevorproject. org/

You can call Trans Lifeline at:-

Suicide Help - Wipe Out Transphobia

www.wipeouttransphobia.com/suicide-help/

Suicide facts and figures from the Samaritans in UK.

https://www.samaritans.org/about-samaritans/research-policy/ suicide-facts-and-figures/

For Vets, or loved ones of Vets; Veterans Crisis Line by call- ing 1-800-273-8255 and Pressing 1. You can also send a text to 838255.

The American Foundation for Suicide Prevention and SAVE (Suicide Awareness Voices of Education).

Numbers often change – So it is better to simply go on the inter- net straight away, to get the latest number to dial or text.

BOOKS OF INTEREST & TRAUMA REFERENCE

Bandler, Richard. And Grinder, John. *Frogs into Princes* (Moab, UT: Real People Press, 1979).

Booty. G. *Chaotic Client & Self – Counselling Skills, Hints & Tips.* (Convergence College of Psychotherapy. Kindle Direct Publishing, 2013).

Booty, G. *Counselling Anxiety, Fears & Phobias – BOOTY'S NOTES, Skills, Hints & Tips.* (Convergence College of Psychotherapy. Kindle Publishing 2019).

Bradshaw, J, *Homecoming – Reclaiming & Championing your inner child.* (Piatkus Books Ltd, London. 1990). The book has sold over three million copies, and one that I really love and encourage everyone to read.

Bradshaw, J. Creating Love. *The Next Great Stage of Growth.* (Bantam Books New York USA. 1992). An excellent follow up book to read.

Carnegie, Dale. *How to stop worrying and start living.* (Cedar and 1998 by Vermilion, Random House Group, London 1953).

Carter, Rita. *Mapping the Mind.* (Weidenfield & Nicolson. London. UK. 1998).

Covitz, Joel. *Emotional Child Abuse* (Boston: Sigo Press, 1986).

Dalzell. R. & Sawyer. E. *Putting Analysis into Child and Family Assessment.* (National Children's Bureau. London & USA. 2007).

Davies, Gaius. *STRESS: The challenge to Christian caring.* (Kingsway Publications. East Sussex. UK. 1989).

Dossey, Larry, M.D. *Recovering the Soul* (New York: Bantam, 1989). ed.This is about the scientific case for the existence of the soul.

Fassel, Diane. *Working ourselves to Death* (SAN Francisco: Harper SF, 1990).

Feinstein, D., Eden, D. & Craig, G. *The Healing Energy of EFT & Energy Psychology.* (Jeremy P. Tarcher / Penguin. USA. 2005).

Fowler, Jeff. *A Practitioners Tool for Child Protection and the Assessment Of Parents.* (Jessica Kingsley Publishers. London. 2003).

Gerhardt, Sue. *The Selfish Society.* (Simon & Schuster UK Ltd. London. 2010).

Gerhardt, Sue. *Why Love Matters* (Routledge. East Sussex England & USA & Canada. 2004).

Grand, David. *Brainspotting The Revolutionary New Therapy For Rapid And Effective Change.* (Sounds True, Inc. Boulder, CO. USA. 2013).

Haley, Jay. *Uncommon* Therapy (New York: W.W. Norton & Co, 1986).

Herman, Judith. L. *Trauma and Recovery.* (Basic Books. USA. 1992).

Hillman, James. *Re-Visioning Psychology* (New York: Harper Collins, 1977). ed. An attempt at pioneering restoration of the soul in today's world.

Johnson, Robert. *Owning Your Own Shadow* (San Francisco: Harper SF, 1991).

Jung, Carl. *Collected Works* (Princeton, NJ: Princeton University Press, 1985).

Kaufman, Gershen. *The Psychology of Shame* (New York: Springer Publishing Co, 1989).

Khazan. Inna. Z. *The Clinical Handbook Of Biofeedback.* (John Wiley & Sons, Ltd. West Sussex. UK. 2013).

Knipe, Jim. *EMDR TOOLBOX* (Springer Publishing Company, New York. 2015).

Lewis, C. S. *The Four Loves* (San Diego, CA: Harcourt Brace Jovanovich, 1971).

Lifting, Robert J. *Thought Reform & the Psychology of Totalism* (Chapel Hill, NC: University of North Carolina Press, 1989).

Lynch, William. *Images of Hope* (Norte Dame, IN: University of Norte Dame Press, 1987). ed. Realistic and fantastic imagination and how it helps understand emotional illness and healing.

Masters. P. *Physician of Souls.* (Wakeman. London, 1976).

Miller, Alice. *The Drama of Being a Child* (Basic Books Inc. and 1987 by Virago Press, Time Warner Book Group, London. 1981).

Miller, Alice. *Thou Shalt Not Be Aware* (a translation of previous work by **Farrar, Straus and Giroux**, Noonday Press. New York. 1984).

Moore, Thomas. *Care of the Soul* (New York: Harper Collins, 1992).

Pastor, Marion. *Anger and Forgiveness* (Berkeley, CA: Jennis Press,

1980).

Parnell, Laurel. *Tapping In* (Sounds True, Inc. Boulder USA. 2008).

Peck, M. Scott. *The Road Les Travelled* (New York: Touchstone / Simon and Schuster, 1980).

Peter. Erik. et. al. *Biofeedback Mastery.* (Association for Applied Psychophysiology and Biofeedback. Wheat Ridge. CO. 2008).

Polatinsky. Melanie. *Life BeyondYour Pain.* (Paradigm Press. South Africa. 1995).

Rogers, Carl R. *On Becoming a Person* (Boston: Houghton Mifflin, 1972).

Rosenberg. Stanley. *Accessing the Healing Power of the Vagus Nerve* (2017. North Atlantic Books California USA).

Rothschild. Babbette. The Body Remembers - Psychophysiology Of Trauma and Trauma Treatment. (W.W. Norton & Company Inc., New York, USA. 2000).

Rothschild. Babbette. *The Body Remembers - Revolutionizing Trauma Treatment.* (W.W. Norton & Company Inc., New York, USA. 2000).

Schore. Allan. N. *Right Brain Psychotherapy.* (W.W. Norton & Company Ltd. USA. 2019).

Sardello, Robert. *Facing the World with Soul* (New York: Lindisfarne Press, 1992).

Stevens, John O. *Awareness* (Moab, UT: Real People Press, 1971). The initiator of my exercise given in training to help understand yourself more by repeating " Who are you?" For you to try to answer the question.

Shapiro, Francine. *Getting Past Your Past* (Rodale Books, USA.

2012). *This is a useful Self Help workbook.

Weinhold, Barry K. and Janae B. *Breaking Free of the Co-Dependency Trap* (Dallas, TX: Still Point Press, 1989).

Welch, Edward. T. *Counselor's Guide to the Brain and Its Disorders.* (Zondervan Publishing House. Michigan USA. 1991). *about the brain from a Christian perspective.

Westbrook, D. Kennerley, H. & Kirk, J. *An introduction to Cognitive Behaviour Therapy Skills and Application.* (SAGE Publications. London. 2007).

Whitfield, Charles. L. *Healing the Child Within.* (Health Communications, Florida, USA. 1989).

Willey, Liane. H. *Pretending to be Normal.* (Jessica Kingsley Publishers, London. 1999). * About Aspergers.

Wolinsky, Stephen. *Trances People Live* (Ashley Falls, MA: Bramble Co, 1991).

Zukav, Gary. *The Seat of the Soul* (New York: Simon and Schuster, 1989).

.

ABOUT THE AUTHOR

Rev Dr George A. Booty

A Senior Faculty Lecturer at 'Convergence College of Psychotherapy' (Organisational members of both CPFI & BACP). Clinical Lead at the 'Lifescript Clinic of Harley Street', London. Also Clinical Lead at Convergence Counselling Services London (CCSL) and Resident Supervisor at the NewStart Service, MK. He also authored several books. George is Psychotraumatologist and Clinical Lead of the Psycho-Trauma Surgery MK and a Member of the  European Trauma org (UKPTS). Listed as Accredited Psychotherapist Member (CPFI). Also on the Accredited Register with the BACP. George is also part of the Expert Witness network in UK. Holding 4 honorary doctorates and International Governor of Peace, recognised by UN and World Peace Org. Speaking engagements: George is available for Public speaking please contact him here. www.convergencecollege.org

Printed in Poland
by Amazon Fulfillment
Poland Sp. z o.o., Wrocław

64196498R00132